Competitive Swimming

An Insider's Guide

Lunn Lestina

Lunn Lestina

ISBN-13: 978-0615633367
ISBN-10: 0615633366

Contents

ABOUT THE AUTHOR

Lunn Lestina is a former world and nationally ranked competitive swimmer. He attended Stanford University on a swimming scholarship, where he and his teammates won the NCAA division I championships for three years in a row, and the PAC 10 championships four times. Before picking Stanford, he had been aggressively recruited by other universities with top-tier swimming programs, including University of Texas, University of Florida, and UCLA.

He specialized in distance freestyle swimming, but participated in and set records in a full range of swimming events as he came up through the ranks of local and club swim meets to reach the NCAA levels. He set multiple local and national records, and is still on the USA Swimming's top 100 list of the all time fastest swimmers.

Lunn Lestina

INTRODUCTION

So you've decided to become a competitive swimmer.

Many proponents of swimming say that this sport is the safest, healthiest sport under the sun. They point out that swimming is low-impact on the joints and muscles and provides a superlative cardio-vascular exercise, lengthening one's lifespan and improving one's quality of life. And if you swim recreationally or casually to "stay in shape," this is most likely true.

But competitive swimming is anything but casual.

Competitive swimmers start to practice daily from a fairly low level. If you are serious and even moderately successful, by the time you are in high school you will be swimming twice a day, six days a week, for several hours each day.

Swimming was my life from a very young age until after I graduated from college. Because of swimming, I had my pick of athletic scholarships from very good colleges – but I was often so exhausted from the 8+ hours a day of workouts that my GPA suffered. Because of swimming, at the age of 43 I am still stronger than most people I know – but I have rotator cuff problems that cannot be fixed and my shoulders sound like grinding gravel. Because of swimming, I had opportunities to go places, see things, and meet people I would not ever had dreamed of otherwise – but I missed out on many of the "typical" high school and college activities because there just wasn't time.

Achieving world class status in any pursuit requires an overwhelming level of dedication and involves some significant risks. It may be the right path for you. It may not be. But you owe it to yourself to think it through, take the risks seriously, be realistic about the rewards, and know as much as you can about what you are getting into before you commit yourself.

Therefore, here is your insider's guide to the real world of competitive swimming. Basically an unvarnished, uncensored full account from an ex world class swimmer, with everything I wish someone had told me or my parents when I was young. The tricks and techniques, the lessons learned, what to embrace and what to avoid. Use it well, and good luck.

Lunn Lestina

SWIMMING STROKES AND TECHNIQUE

There are four distinct competitive swimming strokes: backstroke, breaststroke, butterfly, and freestyle. Many descriptions of these swimming strokes will tell you how they should be done, with long-winded descriptions of each phase of the stroke and what needs to be done where. Unfortunately, swimming is not done in a series of distinct actions. Swimming, like the water in which it's performed, is fluid. Any action taken without proper understanding of the fluid nature of water will slow the swimmer down and take far more energy than necessary. Therefore any discussion of where to place one's head, shoulders, hips, or any other part of the body, is moot without a basic understanding of fluid dynamics.

Many years ago now, at one of the better colleges several physicists were eating lunch around a pool where a practice was being held. As they ate their food, one of them happened to notice a strange occurrence. The point at which a swimmer put his hand in the water and began his stroke was actually behind the point in space where he took his hand out at the end of his stroke. This puzzled the physicists intently. Up to that point, it was thought that a swimmer propelled himself through the water by grabbing a piece of water, climbed along it, like a rung on a ladder, then threw it back behind him at the end of the stroke. Due to the less than solid nature of water, it was thought that the hand should exit the water behind its initial starting point, or at best at the same place. The fact that the hand was exiting the stroke ahead of its starting point flew in the face of their supposed action-reaction Newtonian model of how swimming worked. Something else must be at work.

After some months researching the issue, it was found that the swimmers in question were not using water to push themselves forward, but they were utilizing Bernoulli's Principle to "lift" themselves forward through the water.

When an airplane moves forward, the air moving over the top of its wing moves much faster than the air moving underneath. Slow moving air creates more pressure than air moving quickly so the higher air pressure below the wing causes the plain to experience lift. In a similar way, a swimmers lightly cupped hand creates a hydrofoil shape creating lift in much the same manner.

Now this story may well be apocryphal, but it illustrates well the most important nature of swimming. Everything you do in the sport involves water and how water behaves. Ignore this fact at your peril.

Each swimming stroke, done properly, allows the swimmer to utilize Bernoulli's Principle and other aspects of fluid dynamics to work with the water in creating the most efficient and fastest progress through the water that is possible. Most swimmers don't understand these principles directly but they feel the difference when they're doing it right. Competitive swimmers call this difference a "feel for the water." As we discuss each stroke in more detail, I will try to let you know how a stroke should feel when you're doing it well. Then you'll be closer to finding out what that "feel for the water" is like.

The Swimmer that Made Bernuli's Principle Apparent, Mark Spitz

BACKSTROKE

Backstroke is a descriptive, if not terribly imaginative, term for any stroke that is performed on the back. In fact, US and International Swimming rules for backstroke state just that. As long as the swimmer's shoulders do not break the plane perpendicular to the water's surface at any time, anything goes. You might think that with such a broad definition of the stroke, one might see a number of different approaches to these events. However, over the years of competitive swimming a very distinctive way of moving through the water has emerged.

Test Yourself

Place the backs of your hands together. While leaving the backs of your hands together extend your arms until the insides of your elbows touch. If you can't do it, don't worry, most people cannot.

Those few of you who can, may have a talent at backstroke. Why is this? No one really knows. Some believe that the nature of the stroke allows doublejointed elbows to add an extra push at the end of the stroke. Others think that this backwards bend allows a better placement of the hand at the beginning of the stroke.

Having this particular "advantage" myself, I have developed my own theory. When you're making your first grab for the water at the top of your stroke, a backstroker has to rotate his shoulder down and arm back to get the first feel for the water, or catch. It is my opinion that the extra range of motion that a doublejointed backstroker has allows him a smoother and more extensive catch at the beginning of the stroke. A better catch, leads to a larger differential pressure on either side of the swimmer's hand, generating more power through the rest of the stroke. In other words, the doublejointed backstroker feels like he grabs more water.

Backstroke, being done, of course, on the back, requires a very specific body position. Lay on your back in the pool. If you're not naturally buoyant, then you may need to flutter kick a bit in order to stay afloat. You'll want to imagine a string from your navel reaching all the way to the ceiling holding your belly at the surface of the water. Your head should be tilted backwards so you can see up and back. You should be able to feel the waterline at the very top of your forehead. This body position is the foundation of backstroke. Swimmers who cannot maintain this body position while doing backstroke tend to drop their hips into the water and slow themselves down needlessly.

Backstroke is a rotational stroke, which means that while one side of the body is generating power to move the swimmer forward, the other side is in recovery. More precisely, though, it also means that shoulder roll is terribly important to efficient use of your arms in backstroke. While you're on your back in the water and you've achieved the body position detailed above, begin to flutter kick and roll your shoulders back and forth without letting your arms leave your sides. Now some people hear shoulder roll and think they need to go into a dance routine, but for a backstroker, shoulder roll means simply to bring one shoulder up towards the ceiling and the other down towards the bottom of the pool, then reversing the position. The shoulder that was down, then moves up while the shoulder that was up, moves down. Avoid shrugging. A swimmer whose shoulder roll involves too much shrugging will be seen to "snake" down the pool as they swim.

Now that we've established the foundation of the stroke, we can add the arms. Now if you've read my section on a "feel for the water" you know that swimmers use Bernoulli's Principle of lift in order to move through the water, but when you're swimming, you don't really feel the differing pressures. You feel like you've got a ball of water and you're palming it through the stroke. Anytime you've dropped that ball, your hand will feel a shaking as your hand stalls. Avoid that feeling.

Each pulling motion, or full rotation of the arm, is usually broken down into four phases: the catch, the pull, the release, and the recovery. The foundation of a good pull is the catch. This is where you first find the water "ball" that you'll be using to propel yourself forward. In backstroke, the catch is performed by raising the arm over the head with the pinky finger entering the water first. The shoulder rotates downward allowing the arm to move straight down and the hand to start the first sculling motion of the stroke. It is here that the swimmer first catches the water "ball" that will be used for the entire stroke. I cannot impress enough the importance of a good catch. The water that you get at the beginning of the catch is the water you will be interacting with the entire stroke. The better you catch is, then, the more powerful and efficacious your whole stroke will be.

Now that you have your catch completed we can start using that water to move forward. Once you have your water "ball" at the top of your stroke, you will drop your elbow slightly in order to begin the pull. From this position, palm the water "ball" down towards the bottom of the pool until your hand is even with your shoulder. Next, rotate the "ball" up towards your hip. Once your hand is near your waist, you will reverse the curve of your pull and extend your arm down, straightening the elbow, finishing the stroke down by your thigh.

You will notice that from the start of this pull to the end, we have made a large "S" shape in the water with our hand. This is intentional. To provide the power we need, the hand must make a sculling motion through the entire stroke. While it may feel like we've got a ball of water palmed in our hand, never forget that we're using that water to fly forward. So once you've got the arm rotation of the stroke down, begin to pay attention to your wrist. It is far too easy, for instance to lose power in the middle of your stroke because you've stopped the sculling motion of your hand through your stroke because of the limits of shoulder and elbow range of motion. At these points of the stroke, the top, bottom, and middle sections of your "S" curve, you can be sure to maintain the power of your stroke by simply rotating your wrist a bit. This action keeps the "ball" of water under your control and keeps your stroke power high.

Backstroke Arm Recovery

Once you've finished your stroke at your thigh, it's time to recover the arm for the next stroke. The "ball" of water that we've been using to move forward is now released. Since you're no longer using the water to your benefit with this arm, it needs to exit the water in the most streamlined manner possible. In backstroke, this is accomplished by raising the arm up in time with the shoulder rotation we covered earlier. The shoulder leads the arm up and out of the water and into the recovery phase of the cycle.

Simply put, recovery is when the swimmer gets the arm ready to be used again. In backstroke, the shoulder rotation leads the arm through the entire cycle and in recovery, the arm raises out of the water palm down and is rotated over the head with arms straight. The shoulder rotation at this point should place the arm back into the water over the head, with the pinky in the water first, ready to start our next pull.

Now I know you've probably read many depictions of strokes just like this and are still just as lost as you were before. Well here's how the stroke feels to me when I'm doing it well. My head and neck are isolated while the stroke moves about me. My back feels arched slightly, leaving my chest and stomach at the water's surface the entire time. My shoulders lead every element of my stroke. Each catch finds ample pressure to work with and that pressure on my hand is constant throughout the pull. I'm on a zipline attached to my chest, careening towards my attack on the wall at the other side of the pool.

BREASTSTROKE

Unlike backstroke and freestyle, breaststroke isn't a rotational stroke, it is a iterative stroke. Breaststroke has a power cycle and a glide cycle. This stroke depends greatly upon the timing between the arms and legs in order to porpoise through the water. Breaststroke also has more rules defining its performance than backstroke or freestyle. Every action the swimmer takes must be symmetrical. This means that every action taken by the swimmer must be matched by a mirrored action on the other side of his body. If the kick or arms are uneven at any point, the swimmer is disqualified. Furthermore the swimmers head must break the surface of the water with each stroke. If not, the swimmer is also disqualified.

At earlier times in the stroke's history, this rule has been more strict, stating that the swimmers head must not go below the water at any time. There's an apocryphal story that has been handed down for many years regarding the reason for this ruling. It goes something like this. Early in the days of competitive swimming, there was no such rule regarding keeping ones head at the waterline during breaststroke and it became a stroke that was done almost completely underwater. In fact those that won the breaststroke events breathed as little as possible. Then one world championship sometime in the 1930s, a breaststroker completed an entire 200 meter breaststroke underwater. He won the event, but ended up with brain damage due to the oxygen deprivation. Thus the rule was changed.

Now realistically, this probably never happened, and if it did, it's terribly unlikely that such brain damage was caused just by staying underwater that long. Backstrokers, for instance, these days regularly perform most of their competitive stroke underwater for the same distances and have yet to end up with any detrimental physical effects. I can see, however, how the fear of such an event as a swimmer's injury could lead to the changing of this rule to something like what we use today.

Test Yourself

Measure your torso. If the distance from your shoulders to your hips is close to the distance from your hips to your feet, breaststroke might be your thing.

Several theories have been postulated regarding this fact that people with longer torsos tend to be better breaststrokers than those us who have longer legs. Some believe that the upper body strength of these people tends to be higher, so their breaststroke benefits from this extra power. Others believe that the closer the swimmer's center of gravity is to the head, the easier time the breaststroker will have of getting over the wall of water during the recovery phase of the stroke.

Whatever the reason, a longer torso seems to give an advantage to some breaststrokers.

The arms in breaststroke complete the shortest cycle in competitive swimming. This is the only stroke in which the hands do not finish the power stroke of their cycle by the thigh. The entirety of the arm movement in breaststroke occurs in front of the waistline and some would say even in front of the stomach. To begin the arm motion in breaststroke, lay on your stomach in the water with your head down and your arms over your head. Do not tuck your head against your chest, keep it resting along the water so the waterline rests across the top of your head. Your shoulders will rest against your ears and your hands will be touching at the thumbs in front of your head. As you begin your catch of the water, you will simultaneously raise your head while bringing your hands downwards. Bring your hands perpendicular to the bottom of the pool with the palms facing back towards your feet while keeping your elbows high. Once you feel the balls of water in each of your hands start to create pressure you can begin your pull.

Breaststroke Recovery

The breaststroke pull as we said before, is a very short and fast action. From the initial catch, you will keep your elbows up and bring your hands out to the width of your shoulders while pulling down. Once your hands have reached a point in space under your pectorals, you will start to reverse the outward motion of your pull and bring your hands back into the centerline under your body. As you bring your hands together, you will bring your elbows down under your body and together. This final squeeze of the water underneath your chest brings your pull into the recovery phase. To recover your arms from a breaststroke pull you must be as streamlined as possible. To streamline your recovery, bring your hands and elbows together at your centerline under your body.

As you complete your breath and bring your face back into the water, bring your hands forward until you've reached your catch position.

You may have felt while we perform breaststroke arms without the kick that you have moved backwards while in the recovery phase of your pull. While that might not actually be the case, your forward motion has definitely slowed. Breaststroke is a stroke that, since it is so low in the water tends to push a lot of water around. As such, to perform the stroke at competition speeds, one much find a way to break through or jump over the wall of water you've been building in front of you in the early phases of the stroke. A good and timely kick is the key to doing so.

To practice your breaststroke kick, lay in the water as I described earlier for the pull. Lay prone with your face in the water, the waterline across the top of your head and your hands together over your head with arms at full extension and your thumbs touching. This time your hands will simply stay in place while we focus on the legs. Bring your head up slowly as you bring your feet up towards your bottom by bending your knees together and down towards the bottom of the pool. Take a quick breath as you set your feet into the breaststroke power position. This position may feel a bit odd if you've not done it before so you may want someone to watch for you. From the prone squatting position with your knees down towards the bottom of the pool and your legs and feet together, you will turn both of your feet out so that the toes point out and your heels stay close together. Your knees will want to spread as well but try to avoid this. In one quick motion you will want to bring your feet outside of the line of your shoulders and snap them together at full extension while straightening your legs. As your feet snap together, your breath ends and you'll put your face back into the water. All this is done while making sure your knees are no more than 6 inches apart. A proper breaststroke kick should feel like you have some pressure against the soles of your feet. If not, you are likely pushing with the tops of your feet too much and not keeping your toes out.

Now that we have the pull and the kick down, we'll put the whole stroke together. In order to get over the wall of water that breaststroke generates we'll have to coordinate the pull and kick of the stroke precisely with a streamlined glide. Both parts of the stroke time themselves off of the breath. The beginning of your breath coincides with the catch of the arm stroke. Once the catch is completed and you're starting your pull, the legs move into snap position. At the end of the pull, the kick snap goes off and the head as it completes the breath leads the body down forward through the wall of water created during the earlier parts of the stroke. One trick that top level competitive swimmers do, is a half butterfly kick at the end of the breaststroke kick. This helps reset the body position of the swimmer in a way to best be able to attack the next wall of water. Be careful not to do a complete butterfly kick though, since officials know about this trick and will disqualify anyone who adds an obvious butterfly kick between strokes.

Breaststroke for me feels like I'm rolling over great logs of water. If my timing is off on any part of the stroke, I hit a log wrong, and end up rolling down the back side of it.

BUTTERFLY

For beginners, this is the most demanding and technically precise strokes. If done well, butterfly will feel almost effortless, but if it is done improperly, it will seem like you're swimming in molasses and impossible to move. Like breaststroke, butterfly is an iterative stroke. It has a power cycle and a glide cycle. As such, butterfly requires a very clean and fluid motion in order to be done well. Furthermore, like breaststroke, butterfliers are required to be symmetrical in all their motions. Not only is this a requirement by US and international swimming rules, but it's a good idea from the standpoint of streamlining. Any excess or out of sync movements will greatly diminish your ability to perform butterfly well, if at all.

Butterfly Recovery

All of these cautions can be daunting so let's start with something simple, the butterfly kick. Fly kick starts from the belly. Many instructors talk about hip rotation, but this motion is really the consequence of a good and powerful abdominal movement. While holding your hands in front of you with your thumbs together and arms at full extension, lay prone in the water with the waterline at the top of your forehead. With your feet together, start a wave of your body starting at your belly that runs the length of your body down to your legs. First your stomach will arch downwards, then back up while your pelvis moves downwards, followed by your knees, then your feet. When you get good at the rhythm of this kick, you will feel an almost constant pressure on your feet. The pressure will be on the soles of your feet during the upward motion of the kick and the pressure will be on the tops of your feet during the downward motion of the kick.

Unlike most kicks, most of the effort for the butterfly kick comes from the stomach and back muscles. Given this fact, many butterfliers, and those of us who only did butterfly in Individual Medleys (IMs), had to do hundreds of sit-ups. All-in-all, many swimmers do 500 or so sit-ups every day to get the core of their bodies ready for butterfly kick and freestyle turns. Given that backstroke is done these days with a significant amount of butterfly kick (inverted and underwater, but butterfly nonetheless), this regimen of sit-ups and sit-up variants continues to this day.

Butterfly just won't work without its kick. Oh sure, you can perform butterfly with a pull-buoy but you'll find that you're still kicking during the stroke cycle because it's that necessary to the motion of the rest of the stroke. Therefore it's best to plug the kick right into the stroke as soon as you're ready to work on the arms.

Starting from the prone position with your arms outstretched over your head and your hands shoulder-width apart, begin your catch. This catch is done by bringing your hands perpendicular to the bottom of the pool and keeping your elbows high so that your arms form a large circle around your head. While you begin your pull, perform your first kick. Start tracing the outline of an hourglass with your fingertips keeping your elbows high throughout the stroke. Bring your hands down and slightly outside the line of your shoulders then pull downwards until your hands are even with your shoulders. Then reverse the direction of your pull. Bring your hands in towards your centerline under your belly about four inches apart. At this time perform another kick with the second half of your stroke. Here you will start the bottom half of your hourglass but not finish it. Rotate your hands at the wrists outwards so that you don't let go of the balls of water you got at the catch and extend your arms so that your hands exit the water at your thighs. Now perform the recovery.

Butterfly recovery is one of the more spectacular sights of competitive swimming. Even swimmers who don't do butterfly like to have their picture taken with their arms outstretched over the water. It is an impressive sight. However, if the rest of the stroke up until this point hasn't been done well, you won't have the speed to get there. Your arms come out of the water at the same time as you perform the up stroke of your second kick. Before your next downward kick, those arms must leave the water, you must take your breath, then be reset at the beginning of the stroke, ready to start your catch all over again. Here's how it's done.

Using the momentum from the power phase of the stroke, and a little overbalancing by kicking up against the water, draw your head out of the water. The water level need be no higher than your bottom lip so don't try to lift your body too high. With your shoulders and chin now at the water's surface, lift your arms out of the water at the elbows and once your hands are free of the water, draw your arms in a wide arc around your body. When your hands reach the level of your shoulders, your breath is finished and you will tuck your chin into your chest drawing your head underwater and snapping your hands together over your head. Your hands must knife into the water at the top of the stroke with your elbows slightly bent so that you don't create too much drag during the recovery phase of the stroke. Then you bring your hands into the catch position to start the stroke cycle again.

FREESTYLE

Freestyle is not technically a stroke. It has come to mean a particular stroke that was once called the Australian Crawl, but in reality freestyle is a term meaning the use of any stroke that can get you from one end of the pool to the other. In fact, some swimmers whose butterfly is actually their fastest stroke can, and do, swim freestyle events using their butterfly. The only catch to this choice is that once you've chosen an alternate stroke to use during the freestyle event, you must hold to all the rules regarding that stroke or be disqualified. So while it's rare, but not unheard of, to see people swimming butterfly during a shorter freestyle event, I've never heard of someone trying to do a mile freestyle using butterfly. Freestyle is just easier using the Crawl. Therefore, since the vast majority of swimmers use the Crawl during freestyle events, I'll just call it freestyle from here on out.

Freestyle is done everywhere from the sprinter's 50 to the endurance athlete's 1650, or mile. Other strokes are only done as 100s and 200s. As such, the freestyler can specialize in the distance they find most comfortable. Some coaches, in fact, see the difference in body types and distance specialties of their freestylers and assume that there are differing techniques to sprint freestyle and distance freestyle. The fact is, the stroke is the same, but the attitude is different. Here's how it's done.

Freestyle at Competition

Let's start with the kick. Freestyle, just like backstroke, uses what's called a flutter kick. A flutter kick is an asymmetrical kick where the leg that is kicking down moves opposite the leg that is kicking up. Once the leg has reached the top of its motion it moves down while the other moves up. The full range of motion of the foot in a flutter kick from top to bottom of its cycle is rarely more than twelve inches. If you've ever seen a competitive swimmer do freestyle or backstroke, you'll know what I mean. The trick to a good flutter kick is to always start the kick from the hip, leaving the knees and ankles flexible but firm in their movement of the water. A good kick does not splash. The water should seem to boil. You should feel a constant pressure on the bottoms and tops of your feet as you propel yourself through the water with a good kick and a good kick provides a good foundation for the rest of your stroke.

Like backstroke, freestyle is a rotational stroke. When one arm is creating power for the stroke, the other is in recovery. Thus, like backstroke, a good shoulder roll is very important to a smooth and efficient stroke. However, unlike backstroke, your shoulder roll is the basis for your breathing cycle in freestyle. A swimmer can easily unbalance his stroke by breathing too often to one side or even, when he gets tired, slow down the rotation of his shoulders when he wants to breathe. This shows up often in tired swimmers when they seem to lope down the pool taking short and long strokes as they wind their way down the pool. Now this doesn't mean that swimmer's haven't been

17

successful. In fact some of the best swimmers in the world have had this flaw. High-level competitive swimmers who have this problem, have trained it so deeply into their stroke that their stroke would have to be completely deconstructed in order to fix it. Most coaches just don't bother fixing these issues since they make a living on the speed of their athletes and adjusting a stroke at that level makes the swimmer slower during the relearning process. Nonetheless, an unequal stroke is inefficient and wastes precious energy. Learn it right and train it right so you can be the best you can be.

Lay prone in the water with your arms straight over your head and your thumbs touching. The waterline should be at the top of your forehead. Start your flutter kick. This is the foundation of freestyle. Your arms will move and your shoulders will rotate, but your head, chest and lower body will remain steady. Any movement of the lower body usually means something is out of position in your stroke and means your stroke should be looked at for flaws.

From this position, start your catch. While one arm stays where it is, above your head, bring your fingertips of the other hand down until your hand is perpendicular with the bottom of the pool. Keep your elbow high. Rotate your wrist slightly outward until you feel a ball of water creating pressure on your hand. As you turn your catch into a pull, your shoulder will drop, raising the shoulder of the non-pulling arm a little. Pull the ball of water just outside the width of your shoulder then reverse the flow of the pull back towards the centerline of your body being careful to rotate the wrist out so that you do not lose the ball of water as you change the direction of the pull. Bend your elbow a little more and begin to raise your shoulder back to the beginning, neutral, position while you pull the ball of water under your centerline. Once your hand and the ball of water is under your body, you will reverse the flow of your pull again. Be careful again to not lose the ball of water by rotating your wrist, this time to the inside if your body. Your final push of the stroke now begins. Finish rotating your shoulder back to the neutral position you started the stroke with while bringing the ball of water past your waist and thigh.

Once your hand is at your thigh, your recovery phase with that arm begins. While the catch and pull starts with your other arm, you shoulder will rise, leading the elbow then hand out of the water. Here is where you can take your breath. As your shoulder roll to that side reaches its apex, turn your head just to the side. If you go too far, your kick will have to counterbalance you and you'll see a fast kick out to the side. You won't have to turn very far either, since your progress through the water will create a nice wake in which you will be able to take your breath. Only your mouth need be above water, not your whole head. Once your breath is taken, your arm rolls over your body with its elbow high and fingertips low. Let your shoulder roll return your head to its starting position and knife your hand into the water, finger tips first, about two feet in front of your head at shoulder width. Here you are ready to start the next catch and pull.

The Catch

Freestyle, unlike other strokes really doesn't lend itself to being taken apart very well. Almost all of the motions in the stroke are interdependent upon another. In order to work on differing aspects of the stroke, one drill that I found works well is to use a kickboard in one hand, holding it out in front of yourself while you practice with one arm at a time. Just be sure, as you're doing your freestyle stroke to reach your fingertips a little underneath the kickboard as you start your stroke to simulate the shoulder roll of the other arm as you practice. Another drill that I like to use in order to keep my feel for the water, is sculling.

Sculling is best performed in a prone position with a pull buoy. While your nose is at the waterline, place both arms out in front of you shoulder width apart. Bring your fingertips down so that your hands are perpendicular to the bottom of the pool and your elbows are raised slightly. Using nothing but your wrists and hands, scull, moving your hands back and forth and propel yourself to the other end of the pool. Not only does this drill give you an excellent feel for the water, it teaches you how to catch the water at the beginning of a stroke easily and efficiently. You may get a little tired at first, but the results are worth it, especially when you sprint.

Some coaches mistakenly have the belief that sprinting and distance freestyle are two different strokes that require different disciplines to do well. Don't get me wrong, there are a number of differences between the swimmers that can do these events well. Sprinters tend to be well-built muscular individuals with an ability to go into deep anaerobic deficit. Distance swimmers, however, are pure aerobic athletes. Both freestylers, however benefit greatly from an efficient stroke and you can do them both as well with the following mindsets.

When you sprint freestyle, your job is to get to the end as fast as possible. No one who did the best they could in a sprint ever bothered to take a breath. Furthermore, as a sprinter, you don't have the luxury of finding your feel for the water with every stroke. When you start your catch, do your best to grab all the water you can, but don't wait on the perfect grab. The sprinter's catch moves so fast into their pull that there really isn't any separating the two. If sprinting is your thing, be sure to practice your catch quickly so that you will have the most power through your stroke. Furthermore, a sprinter's kick is powerful. Since the sprinter is going to go into deep anaerobic deficit anyway, there's no point in holding back anything so power your kick as hard as you can without splashing. Then you'll be sure to get as much out of your stroke as possible.

Unlike sprinting, distance swimming is all about efficiency and everything you can do to work with the water to maintain your aerobic strength is key. A distance freestyler's stroke is a little longer then a sprinter's. You'll have time to work with your catch so that you're as efficient as possible. Keep focused on your body position so that you don't work against yourself and breathe. Many distance swimmers end up breathing every other stroke which is fine as long as you don't get unbalanced. If you feel yourself starting to lope down the pool with uneven strokes, switch to breathing to the other side a bit. Another tip for a distance swimmer, is never ever wear a cap if you can help it. Endurance athletes lose a terrible amount of effectiveness if they overheat and you can dissipate a lot of heat through your head without a cap to keep it in.

Ok, I can hear you saying, all these tricks are nice and I'll take years trying to figure out just how to do the stroke you just described, but how does a good freestyle feel? Well, I'll tell you. In freestyle, more than any other stroke, your heart leads the way. This is why, when my freestyle feels right, I feel like my heart is pulling me forward through the water like a love-sick teenager pining after their latest crush. It's not very scientific, but many excellent freestylers describe the stroke as being powered by their love for the sport. The body position engendered by this feeling really is optimal, I think, for a good freestyle. Try it.

TURNS

Turns are violence. Many non-competitive swimmers will wonder what I mean by this statement since swimming is such a beautiful and non-violent sport. It's elegant and graceful since water is the only thing you can use to move yourself and water will resist any violent movement. Hah. You've never seen a good flip turn then. In reality every good turn is violent. Imagine a ball being thrown against the side of a house. The harder you throw that ball, the faster it will come back to you. Well in swimming, you're the ball. The faster you hit that wall, the faster you'll come off it, and the faster will be your time.

In this section I will describe the timing, action, and feel of good turns. It's not for the faint-hearted. Even the best swimmers have had their concussions, dislocations, and broken bones trying to do these turns well, but in the end it's worth it. Who doesn't want a faster time anyway?

BACKSTROKE TURNS

Of all the turns in swimming backstroke turns have changed the most over the past 15 years. Considering the present state of the rules, it is likely that this turn will change further due to some fairly ambiguous rulings as they stand now. Originally, the turn required a swimmer to touch the wall with their hand before initiating the turn, which needed to be done completely on the back (with the shoulders not passing the vertical plane). This turn looked a lot like a turtle spinning on its back. An innovation by backstrokers in the early 1980s altered this turn by having the touching hand reach across the body to initiate a very crabbed freestyle turn on the side. While the shoulders never broke the vertical plane, it led to a number of confused officials mistakenly disqualifying backstrokers until they got used to it. Some barked ankles, and broken ankles later, led the swimming powers that be to change the ruling yet again so that the hand need not touch the wall during the backstroke turn. Furthermore, to possibly ease the nerves of confused turn judges, the backstroker was allowed to make a full flip over on to the stomach in order to prepare for what was now essentially a freestyle turn in a backstroke event. This rule change has led to the first of two fungible aspects to the ruling on backstroke turns.

Test Yourself

Do you have a small nose or long lips? If you do it may help your backstroke.

In the late 80s when the art of using a butterfly kick underwater was being developed, we found that those of us who could purse our lips and effectively block off our nostrils had an advantage. They didn't lose as much air as others did when kicking on our backs underwater. Now that you can only go 15 meters underwater it might not matter quite so much but the best swimmers still push the boundaries. If you have any physical advantage, use it.

The swimmer is now allowed to take one full stroke as their body passes through the vertical plane to prepare for the flip turn. Now if you've ever misjudged your distance to the wall in a backstroke turn before you know you might end up gliding a bit before being able to initiate your turn. Well this is now a no-no. If your rotation onto your stomach is an anyway too long or stops in a glide before you initiate your turn, you're going to be disqualified. However, what's a glide and what's a long roll is in the eye of the beholder, so beware. In my experience most judges will just institute a one-second rule on this. If they can count, "one Mississippi," before you start your turn, you'll get disqualified.

The second area where there's some flexibility in the backstroke turn rules is how far you're able to go underwater before your head has to break the surface. In the late 1980s some swimmers were swimming the length of the pool underwater using butterfly kick before taking a few strokes to prepare for their turn then swimming underwater again to the flags on the other side of the pool. This innovation forced swimming's timid rulemakers to restrict the distance that a person can swim underwater before their head must break the surface. At first this distance was 10 meters, double the distance that backstroke flags are installed from the wall, but when most high-level swimmers blew past that distance regularly underwater, the distance was extended to 15 meters. Now 15 meters is farther than half-way down a short course pool so judging that distance shouldn't be a problem for NCAA swimming, but in long course, where most pools are outdoors, that's a different matter. In lower-level events where coaches are able to be on the deck, you should be able to stand someone at the side of the pool where the 15 meter mark is. However in more important events, you're going to have to measure and mark off some landmark of the pool that will work for you. At present there are no markings that are required of pools to define this 15 meter mark. In fact, the suggestion to referees, by US Swimming is that they use their judgment. This means, guess.

Backstroke Streamline

My suggestion in regarding to all these rules is do your best to stay within them but it's your time that matters so push these boundaries to their limit. Measure off and practice your strokes to the wall from the flags and find landmarks that are just within the 15 meter mark from the wall, and use them. Then if you make an innovation that forces another rule change? Good for you.

At present the backstroke turn is very much like a freestyle turn. The only real difference is that you start and end the turn on your back. Of course when you're on your back, you set up your turn very differently than when you're prone, so let's start there. Most backstrokers are taught their turn approach starts at the flags. While this is a handy and useful way of judging your distance to the wall, most of the top swimmers in the world use their stroke count from the entire length. They also know that they have a different number of strokes to complete a length of the pool from their first length than on their second length. However, as you're getting used to doing this turn, a stroke count from the flags to the wall will do for now.

To find out how many strokes it takes for you to get from the flags to the wall, swim one length backstroke. Once you've reached the flags, start counting. For a 10 year old or so, the stroke count can be as high as 8 strokes. For an adult in good swimming form, it can be as few as 2 and a half strokes. You may hit your head the first time, and that's ok. Just take your stroke count and subtract one. Now that you have your stroke count to the wall from the flags, you're ready to attack the wall. Your last stroke before the wall will be a long one that rolls you over from your back to your front. As your arm moves in front of your face, you will dive your head around that arm so that your bottom is close to the wall, but both your feet and head are not. Then with all your might, you will snap your legs over your body to hit the wall with as much force as you can muster. As soon as your feet contact the wall, you explode away on your back in a streamlined position with your arms locked together over your head and your chin tucked against your chest.

Hold this streamlined position for a little bit. Starting your butterfly kick too early will slow you down so you have to judge when you're moving slightly slower than you would if you were just kicking underwater. Then start your kick. As we discussed in the butterfly section, the butterfly kick starts just under the ribcage and rolls down the body to the feet. Kick so that you feel pressure on the tops and soles of your feet constantly and start to watch for your 15 meter guidepost without losing your streamlined position. Ideally, you want to hit the surface of the water just at this mark. Once you're close to the surface of the water, you will take the most important stroke of the length of the pool. This is the stroke that instantly returns you to proper body position and rockets you through the surface tension of the water that you'd been avoiding up to this point by being underwater. Feel for the water at the top of your stroke and make sure you've got a really good ball to pull on. Then with a massive pull, break the surface of the water and put your head into proper position for backstroke. At the same time, take your last and most powerful butterfly kick. Start your second pull a little early as well to continue with the breakthrough motion.

BREASTSTROKE TURNS

Unlike freestyle and backstroke turns, where you hit the wall once during your turn, breaststroke turns require you to touch the wall twice in the act of turning. US and international swimming rules dictate that a breaststroker must touch the wall with both hands evenly at the start of each turn and at the end of the race. So if a freestyle turn is like throwing a ball at a wall, a breaststroke turn is like having to hit two walls with that ball before catching it. Physics is working against you. Competitive swimmers, however, have found a way to make this process as elegant and efficient as possible while obeying the rules to the letter. Here's how it's done.

Since you have to hit the wall with your hands, it's very important for you to hit the wall at the most opportune phase of the stroke. If you hit too late, you'll end up gliding your way to the wall with no momentum to drive into the wall for the turn. You end up having to almost climb out of the water in order to get your feet on the wall for your push-off. If you hit the wall too early, you'll have to take a half-stroke to get your arms into position on the wall. Such a stutter-stroke forces action on the water that it resists and steals your momentum as well. Optimally, you will want to hit the wall during your arm recovery just after your kick has started. If you recall when I spoke of breaststroke feeling like you're rolling over and under great logs of water, the point at which you want to hit the wall is just after rolling over the last log of water before the wall. You will feel like you're hitting the wall downhill enabling you to drive that momentum into the rest of your turn.

Once you've hit the wall with both hands evenly, you're ready to redirect the energy you brought to the wall into your breaststroke turn. Immediately upon hitting the wall, bring your left hand down to your hip and drop your left shoulder while tucking your knees under your body. Your momentum from your hands hitting the wall will carry your feet to the wall as you spin about your center of mass. As your feet near the wall, throw your head to your left shoulder and bring your right hand to your right ear. Now, while retaining as much momentum as possible from your original contact with the wall, drive your feet through the wall and explode into a full streamline. This is the fastest you will go while doing breaststroke and retaining this speed is key.

Hold your streamline until you feel the water moving along your body slow to somewhere near the speed of your surface breaststroke. A common error that many swimmers make is to start their stroke too early either because of being tired or out of breath. You're simply slowing yourself down. Once you feel your speed has reached that just below that of your normal breaststroke speed, start your underwater pull. Unlike all breaststroke done at the surface, your hands are allowed to go all the way down to your hips. Make the most of it. Starting from the streamlined position with your hands locked over your head and your head tucked against your chest, catch the water. While keeping your head tucked against your chest, separate your hands to shoulder-width apart and feel for a good catch of water.

Feel the balls of water in your hands, telling you you're using Bernoulli's Principle well. Once you've got a good huge mass of water to work with, rotate both hands out from the midline of your body while keeping your elbows up. Continue to keep your elbows high while bringing those balls of water even with your head. As you bring those balls of water under your body, you will feel the need to roll your body over it. Go with it.

In the past, breaststrokers have been forbidden to use any dolphin kicks during the stroke at all. These rules probably stem from the fact that breaststroke and butterfly were once the same stroke and a distinction had to be made between the two to make them distinct again. The fact remains, though, that both strokes are quite similar in their approach and a certain amount of common actions are necessary to best flow with the water. This commonality has revealed itself in the most recent rule adjustment to breaststroke involving the performance of one butterfly kick during the underwater breaststroke pull. For a long time this kick was forbidden and breaststrokers had to keep their body straight during their underwater pull. This rigid style worked against the water and against the breaststroker's speed, so competitive swimmers began to work around it.

At first, the breaststrokers were merely rolling their bodies around the pull as they brought the water down past their chest and hips, being very careful to keep their legs still. However, as swimmers became more adept at rolling around the water they were pulling on, and the action became faster, it become harder and harder for officials to determine whether a butterfly kick was being done or whether the swimmer was merely working with the water to increase their underwater speed. So to make life easier on the officials, the rule was changed to allow for one butterfly kick during the underwater pull phase of the breaststroke event. Now a full butterfly kick is allowed, but many swimmers now try to over use it and reduce their momentum through the water accordingly. Don't make this mistake.

As you bring the balls of water under your head, untuck your head and tuck it again around the water as your hands come even with your shoulders. Now reverse the rotation of the water back towards the centerline of your body. If you start to lose the balls of water, feel free to rotate your wrists slightly to keep the flow of water constant. Rotate your hands back under your belly and bring your hips up as your roll around the balls of water that you have been working with. Once your elbows are at your sides and your hands are under your belly, you'll reverse the flow of your pull once again. Isolate your elbows at your sides and caress the water down past your thighs rotating your hands to your thighs. As the ball of water you were working with at the beginning of your underwater stroke passes your knees finish your butterfly kick upwards and glide again until you've reached a speed close to that of your normal breaststroke.

Recover your arms into the breaststroke catch position. This hand recovery is performed by bringing your hands together under your body and crossing them over each other with your elbows tight at your side. Once your hands are under your face, raise your head and dive your hands into your first breaststroke catch on the surface. Ideally you will be just at the surface at this point and your head will break the surface at just this time. Feel for the surface of the water with the back of your shoulders. It should feel a little less dense and more like ripples as you get close, but you shouldn't feel air. There really is no trick to timing your stroke to break the surface at the right time besides practice.

I know it seems like a lot to digest, but the breaststroke turn is really one of the easier turns to master if timed correctly. It's all about conservation of momentum. So when you're doing a breaststroke turn well, it feels a lot like a good jazz tune. You hit the wall with a good downbeat, your head and hands perform a syncopated upbeat and the underwater pull, recovery and first stroke flow from there.

BUTTERFLY TURNS

Butterfly and breaststroke share a common history so it's no surprise that they share a turn. Aside from the approach to the wall and the takeoff, butterfly turns are exactly the same as breaststroke turns. Like breaststroke, butterfly requires a swimmer to touch the wall with both hands evenly at the end of each length of the pool. With the need to hit the wall twice during this turn, once with the hands for the rules requirement and once with the feet to push off from the wall, a swimmer must maintain as much momentum through the process as possible in order to execute the butterfly turn well. So like breaststroke turns, butterfly turns must be begun at the proper phase of the stroke in order to drive as much momentum into the turn as possible.

The best phase to contact the wall during a butterfly turn is at the very end of the arm recovery but before the catch. If you reach the wall too late, you'll end up gliding your way to the wall and have no momentum to carry yourself through the rest of the turn. A swimmer who reaches the wall too late in their stroke rotation will look like they're climbing out of the pool during their turn in order to bring their feet to the wall. If you reach the wall too early in your stroke rotation, you will be approaching the wall too slow and too low for your momentum to carry through to your feet when it comes time to drive off the wall. Considering how important first contact with the wall is in a butterfly turn, you might wonder how competitive swimmers hit the wall in this sweet spot so consistently. They count their strokes.

Some swimmers count every stroke in a length. While this is fine for top-notch swimmers in short course (25 yard pool) events who take between eight and twelve strokes per length, it gets a bit much to count for a long course (50 meter pool) event. In this case, most butterfliers start counting their strokes from the flags. How might a swimmer use the flags during their butterfly turns? Most lane lines in competition pools change color at the flags. This color change is what competitive swimmers watch for. Once you know how many strokes you take from the flags to the wall, you can slightly lengthen or shorten your strokes in order to hit the wall at precisely the sweet spot of your arm recovery in order to drive as much momentum into your butterfly turn as possible.

Once you've hit the wall, you're ready to redirect the energy you brought to the wall into your turn. Immediately upon hitting the wall, bring your left hand down to your hip and drop your left shoulder while tucking your knees under your body. Your momentum from your hands hitting the wall will carry your feet to the wall as you spin about your center of mass. As your feet near the wall, throw your head to your left shoulder and bring your right hand to your right ear. Now, while retaining as much momentum as possible from your original contact with the wall, drive your feet through the wall and explode into a full streamline.

Hold your streamline until you feel the water moving past your body is just under that of your normal butterfly speed then begin your kick. The kick needs to start slow and small and work its way larger and stronger as you near the surface. You will feel yourself near the surface of the water as the water moving over your shoulders and back starts to feel less dense. If you've waited until you feel ripples on your back, you've waited too long. Here, you break the surface tension of the water for the first time so it's important that you make this stroke the most powerful of the length of the pool. Break your streamline as you reach the surface by moving your hands to shoulder width and feel for the balls of water under your hands. Slowly bring your head up out of its tucked position and drive into your first stroke.

A good butterfly turn, much like a good breaststroke turn, is a double hit. You dive down on to the wall from the top of your stroke, punch the wall, then drive off as hard as you can. The finesse in this turn is all in the timing of the first hit, if you get that right, the rest of the turn is easy.

FREESTYLE TURNS

Races are won and lost at the walls, freestyle especially so. A good freestyle turn can charge your next length of the pool with momentum. A poor turn, can rob you of that same momentum, making you waste energy during the rest of the length trying to make up your lost ground. Furthermore, since freestyle is done at greater distances than other strokes, an efficient freestyle turn becomes critical in maintaining your energy in those endurance races. I know when you're watching expert freestylers do their turns; it can seem baffling as to how the flip turn is performed. As one watches the turn, the swimmer approaches, the wall, there's a splash and a blur of feet, then the swimmer is streamlined underwater in what seems like an instant. It's all very fast, but that's the point isn't it?

Some unknowledgeable coaches describe a freestyle turn as a summersault in the water followed by a push off of the wall and a corkscrew to return to the prone (face down) position. This is not only wrong, but terribly inelegant. A freestyle flip turn is just that, a flip, and all connotations to speed and explosiveness apply.

Judging the Approach to the Wall

A good freestyle flip turn starts with the approach to the wall. Every stroke's turn has a sweet spot where hitting the wall is optimal and the freestyle flip turn is no different. What's unique about the freestyle turn, though, is you only ever touch the wall with your feet, not your hands first like in butterfly or breaststroke (or even the really old backstroke turns). So you really won't know if you've hit your sweet-spot in your approach until well after you've started your flip. All competition pools have some sort of line on the bottom of the pool. Sometimes this line ends in a "T" sometimes it doesn't, but this is the best gauge to determine where you should start your turn. Since every pool is different, you'll need to establish during your warm up before the event what cues you will be using to determine the start of your freestyle turn.

Here's a drill that worked for me as I was getting used to a new pool. Approach the wall, at speed, using freestyle and start your turn. Have your feet contact the wall, but do not push off. If your feet touch the wall with your knees bent, or if your heels hit the top of the wall, you're too close. Keep lengthening the distance you turn from the wall until your feet hit the wall with your knees bent slightly in the proper place for a push-off. Once you've found your sweet spot, do the turn again and watch to see where your hand crosses the "T" at the end of the pool during your catch. Do not move your head around to find it, you will lose momentum. Once you see where your hand crosses that "T" you have your cue for your turn to start.

As your arm moves in front of your face, on your last pull over the "T", you will dive your head around that arm so that your bottom is close to the wall, but both your feet and head are not. Then with all your might, you will snap your legs over your body to hit the wall with as much force as you can muster. This extension from the waist is the flip. Make sure you've done enough sit ups to prepare your body for this action or you will injure your back. As soon as your feet contact the wall, explode away on your side in a streamlined position with your arms locked together over your head and your chin tucked against your chest.

Hold your streamline until you feel that your speed has become just less than that of your regular freestyle stroke speed. Then begin your kick, first lightly, then with more driving force as you feel the water above your shoulders start to thin. When you feel you're near enough to the surface of the water, start your first pull. Feel for your first catch and be sure to make it a good one. Un-tuck your head and move it into the forward-looking freestyle position. Start your second pull a little early to make sure you've powered through the surface tension of the water and take your first breath which brings me to my next point.

Never breathe near the wall. The wall is the only solid thing you're allowed to contact during a swimming event, and as such will provide you with the greatest opportunity to add speed and momentum to your stroke. When you breathe going into or coming out of your freestyle turn, you rob yourself of valuable momentum. Don't do it.

In competitive swimming, the freestyle flip turn is an integral part of the chess match that goes on during an event. I'm sure you've heard of swimmers drafting each other during freestyle events. There are two places that a swimmer can draft effectively while in another lane. The first is at the shoulder of the other swimmer. The wake coming off the lead swimmer creates a trough for the second swimmer to set in, costing the lead swimmer energy. The second is just at the lead swimmer's waist. Here the end wake from the lead swimmer's feet creates another wake for another swimmer to use. Swimmers who are evenly matched in terms of speed and conditioning will duel over who is drafting whom.

What's special about flip turns, is you can't draft during them. A powerful flip turn at an unexpected time can dislodge that otherwise equal swimmer from swimming in your wake, making the surprised swimmer waste energy during the next lap catching up, driving you ahead to clear water and the win. Or, if you're the one drafting, you can use the turn to jump ahead of your competition when they're not paying attention and tired form the energy you've been leaching from them.

STARTS

If swimming feels like you're flying through the water, the start is your takeoff. Unlike an airplane, though, you are not allowed to use a runway. All swimming starts begin from a full stop. From this dead stop you will have to create all the momentum you will ever get in an instant. Swimmers commonly think of the start as an explosion or the release of a coiled spring, and in short distance events where a good start is the difference between winning and losing, that's exactly what it's like. So let's get inside the head of a competitive swimmer and see what a world-class start is like from the inside.

Takeoff

Before we get into the mechanics of the start, let's look at the starter, the official that starts every race. Part of the starter's duties is to announce the event right before calling the swimmers to their marks. Considering the large number of heats that the starter has to announce, call to their marks, and start, it's a rare individual indeed that does not fall into a cadence. World-class swimmers will watch for this rhythm, observe it, and plan their starts accordingly.

Starters the world over are taught to bring the swimmers to their marks then wait for every swimmer to stop moving before starting the race. A full heat of swimmers who are experienced enough to watch for the starter's cadence will come to their marks quickly so as to not interrupt the starter's rhythm. A swimmer who does not, will throw everyone off. This can be to a sprinter's advantage however, if they are confident they will not be caught off guard by the starter's broken-cadence start. A starter who feels manipulated by a swimmer will be extra vigilant as well, so if you want to try this tactic, be very sure your start is flawless.

A starter will either use a starter's pistol, which will require replacing spent cartridges and constant oiling in order to function in the damp environment of a pool, or a button that starts an automatic timing system. To substitute for the starter pistol's flash, automatic timing systems come equipped with a strobe light that flashes at the same time as the starters beep. Either way, it is the flash, and not the sound of the starter's device that starts the race. Some swimmers have watched the finger of the starter to get a jump on the competition, but since both gun and button can be partially engaged without starting the race this strategy has led to more than a few false starts.

A false start occurs when a starter feels that either a swimmer has started a race without coming to a complete stop, or they feel that a swimmer has started early. A swimmer may not have actually started early. They may have just timed their start expertly, but reality is not important here, the starter's opinion is. If the starter feels that a false start has taken place, they will call the swimmers back by repeatedly shooting the pistol or holding down the starting button which will emit a repeated beeping. If the swimmers don't notice the false-start signal, a rope is usually engaged. This rope, called the false-start rope, is strung across the pool at roughly the half-way mark. When a false start occurs, it is dropped into the pool to notify swimmers that their race has been recalled.

Assuming there is no false start, the starter will bring you to the pool with the following announcement, "Swimmers, this is 50 yards freestyle, two lengths of the pool."

At this point you are on the block, feeling lose, and breathing deeply to suffuse your body with oxygen since you will not be breathing at all during this event. Remember the starter's cadence you've studied up to now and start replaying it in your mind. You are standing two feet back from the front of the block and ready to be called to your marks. The starter calls you to, "take your marks."

You step forward into your starting position, feet shoulder-width apart. If you prefer a foot back position you leave your off foot back, with the toes even with the back of your front foot's heel. Your front foot has its toes curled over the front edge of the starting block. If you prefer a double foot style, both feet are brought to the front of the starting block with their toes curled over the edge of the block. Bring your head down to your knees and touch the front of the starting block with the balls of your hands. As the cadence timing you observed earlier brings to a close bring your back and bottom muscles taught without moving at all on the outside and watch for the flash.

Release.

All the tension you've built up to this point is released in an explosion of effort. From your doubled-over position, explode straight out over the pool, reaching for the other side. Push with your feet against the front of the starting block with the toes you had curled over the edge, made all the more powerful from your arms flying out fast in front of your body. Newtonian physics makes the effort you put into raising your arms forward without bending your elbows drive your feet harder against the starting block than you could with your legs and back alone. For a short moment you are flying.

Fill yourself from the navel to the neck with the only air you will get for the next 18 seconds. This is a sprint after all and breathing will only make you slower. As you feel your airspeed begin to slow, bend slightly at the waist and get ready to enter the water. Feel your fingertips enter the water and tuck your head so your chin touches your chest. Just after entering the water with your head, arch your back. Your hips and feet follow your chest through the smallest hole you can make with your body into the water, avoiding unwanted surface tension drag. Hold your streamline until you begin to match the speed of your stroke, and start swimming.

The momentum derived from your explosion off the starting blocks is maintained through streamlining and as little contact with the surface of the water as possible. You should feel like you've lead the swimmers off the blocks and anticipated the starter perfectly. Upon entering the water, no resistance or shaking of the water should be felt.

BACKSTROKE STARTS

Backstroke, as its name implies, must be done on the back. Given this fact, backstroke starts cannot be done from a starting block the same way that all other strokes are. You must start on your back. In order to be positioned this way from the beginning of the race, the backstroker starts from in the water with their back facing the opposite end of the pool. Now this may seem to be a terribly complicated way of starting a race, but in reality, once you know what you're doing, it's far easier to do a backstroke start well than a normal start.

Let's start with the basics. Jump in the pool in front of the starting blocks. After you come to the surface, face the starting blocks. You'll notice that underneath the starting block platform there are handles. Place your hands on these handles approximately shoulder-width apart and put your feet up on the wall, just underneath the water level. When the starter says, "take your marks," you will add more potential energy to your start by pulling yourself towards the starting block with your arms. From this point, it is remarkably easy to just let go when you see the flash from the starter's signal beginning the race. Reaction time, however, is not the hardest part of this start, since even the slowest of us can drop a ball on cue. It's how you set your feet that makes all the difference.

The Backstroke Start

The balls of your feet create most of the force you get from this start. However, as you pull yourself up to the starting position in this start, you create a significant amount of shearing force on the area where the balls of your feet meet the wall of the pool. So if your feet have to be on vinyl, tile, or metal in the slippery environment of a swimming pool, there is a real chance you will lose your footing and waste all the energy of your start. Slipping wasn't always a problem though.

Before starting rules were standardized, backstrokers were allowed to use the gutters on many pools to aid in their starts. They'd curl their toes over the gutter in order to get a better purchase for their start. In fact, some backstrokers, would not even enter the water at all before the race, preferring to start standing up in the gutter while holding on to the sides of the starting block platform instead. Unfortunately, the days of these elegant starts are done now that US and International Swimming rules state that all backstrokers must start with their toes underneath the water level and never curl their toes over the gutter even when the water level is above the edge of the gutter. I cannot hazard a guess as to why this rule has been put in place but since it has, backstrokers have to look to their ingenuity in order to work around it.

Some backstrokers, simply lower their angle of attack to the wall in order to avoid slipping. Instead of pulling themselves up to their marks, they pull themselves directly toward the starting blocks. A start like this is terribly flat and shallow compared to those that once used the gutter to great advantage. Another way that some backstrokers handle this issue is to set their feet below the waterline, pull themselves up at the starter's mark, and once the starting signal is given, quickly place their feet on the gutters, then start normally. While this solves the problem of slipping feet, it adds another beat before the backstroker can start and in some cases, a slower start is worse than a bad start. One way to solve this problem is to borrow a trick from the minor leagues of the sport and use pine tar.

Now you might wonder if I had suddenly changed subjects to baseball, but like baseball there are small organizations of summer swimming teams dotted all over this country. Here is where many swimmers get their start into the world of competitive swimming and many of these swimmers never make it any farther, but they in their circumstances make some of the most interesting innovations to the sport. For instance, few, if any, of these summer pools can afford starting blocks, so all starts happen from the side of the pool, which is terribly close to the water for someone used to starting from blocks. Furthermore, with no starting blocks, the backstrokers have to use their teammates to be their starting blocks. Their simple and elegant solution to the lack of starting blocks is to have their teammate stand at the edge of the pool with their backs to the water. This teammate is called the backstrokers, "legs," and legs are what they use. Instead of using the handles underneath a starting block the backstroker simply pulls themselves into starting position by pulling on their teammate's legs.

Now even with these "legs" the backstrokers in these summer leagues have the same problem with their feet slipping that backstrokers at the higher levels of the sport have. What was their solution? They used a variation on the baseball player's pine tar called pine oil. Pine oil is a tacky substance used to paint the hooves of horses for equestrian events and is available at any tack shop. It is a non-water-soluble, tacky substance that can be painted on the balls of the feet then washed off with soap and water (or turpentine if you really want to be clean). I suspect that this innovation was adapted from another sport because swimmers at this level of competition are rarely just swimmers. They compete in many other forms of athletics as well and the commonly used equipment in one sport was easily adapted to swimming. The fact remains though that it worked.

With the pine oil on their feet these summer-league swimmers were able to execute better starts. They were able to pull themselves higher on the wall, add more potential energy to their start, and go farther in the air above the surface of the water than their opponents, which is exactly how the start is supposed to be done. With the added friction of your feet on the wall, pull yourself up into the starting position. At the starter's signal, let go of the starting block and turn your palms facing up while dropping your head back. The palms-up orientation of your hands makes it easy to bring your arms straight outside your body, as if you were doing an upside down butterfly recovery. Explode off the wall using the enhanced traction of your feet to arch your body backwards through the air. As your arms come over your head, stretch them into a full-streamline position with your head tucked against your chest just as your fingertips enter the water.

The act of tucking your head into the streamline position just as you enter the water will reverse your arch. Breaking the surface tension of the water in as small an area as possible is an important key to any good start so be sure not to flop or smack the water in any way as you enter the water. As your arch reverses itself under water, watch for your depth under water and adjust accordingly. Hold your streamline until your water speed is just under that of your normal backstroking speed, and begin your underwater butterfly kick. Feel the pressure stay constant on the bottom and tops of your feet as you start kicking lightly and crescendo your kick in strength as you approach the water's surface near the fifteen meter mark. When you're approximately a hand's-width underwater, begin your first stroke. Separate your hands to shoulder-width apart and feel for your first catch. As you begin your catch, roll your shoulder down into the first stroke and break the surface of the water with all the power you can muster. The surface tension of the water is your enemy and you want to power through it on every start and turn.

A good backstroke start feels like flight, even more so than a normal start. As you leave the blocks flying in a direction you cannot see, you know the water is there, but part of you always wonders a little so the sense of free-fall is a lot more prevalent. It's both a relief and a burden to return to the water after your short flight through the air since you've just started a period of time when you cannot breathe and your orientation to the surface of the water pulls the air out of your body. Yet, once you begin your return to the surface of the water for your first stroke, your instincts that have been trained into your body over years of practice take over and you get down to the business at hand of preparing for your first turn.

It's been a terribly long time since I had anything to do with summer league swimming so there may be yet other products like pine oil that can be used to help a backstroker's start. The ability to add friction to a water-soaked environment is hardly a new need. So experiment. I'm sure you'll find your own ingenious methods of handling this problem.

RELAY STARTS

Momentum is speed. Most starts only allow you to generate your momentum at the split instant of the starter's signal, but the start of the second, third, and fourth legs of a relay race are very different. Here the only thing that matters is that your feet continue to touch the starting blocks until the previous swimmer touches the wall. Any movement that you take up and to this point is fair game. So while running starts are not allowed, another method of adding momentum to your start has been developed solely for relay starts. Here's how it's done.

While you watch your teammate approach the wall on their final lap of their race take your position on the starting block. As with a normal start, place your feet at the edge of the block with your toes curled over the front edge, with your feet shoulder-width apart. Now instead of coming to your marks and a full-stop at the edge of the platform, you will need to watch your teammate approach the wall. US and International Swimming rules state that your feet cannot leave the starting blocks until your teammate has touched the wall so your feet cannot move once set. However, nothing precludes using the rest of your body to your advantage.

Getting Ready to Start a Relay Leg

With your feet set at the edge of the starting block, bend at the waist and flex your knees slightly. Extend your arms in front of you with your hands about 6 inches apart and sight through your hands at your teammate approaching the wall. As he comes underneath the backstroke flags bend your knees and at your waist a little more and get ready to spring away. As your teammate takes his last stroke, quickly windmill both your arms over your head, around behind your body, past your waist, and stop suddenly in front of you. The momentum created by this windmill will almost launch you off the blocks all by itself. So when you add this momentum to an explosion with your legs off of the starting blocks you've really got some power off the blocks.

The only possible problem with this start is in the timing. If the swimmer in the water takes a breath inside the flags, you'll likely end up disqualified because the swimmer on the blocks needs to time his touch without actually being able to see it. The goal in all relay starts is to be fully laid-out over the water, while the other swimmer is just touching the wall. Anything less is wasted time.

SWIMMING EQUIPMENT

I can just hear some of you thinking, "this'll be a short section." After all, swimmers do their sport practically nude. They have no shoes, helmets, pads, or other items to worry about during their events so all we'll need is a short description of the suits and we'll be done, right? You couldn't be more mistaken.

Swimmers on the whole depend upon a significant amount of support equipment that never makes it into the pool with them. Some equipment they use in the pool but you cannot see because it's invisible, and some equipment is so small that you hardy take notice. Other items are obvious. So what makes a good swimsuit or a good set of goggles? What hidden items do swimmers use? What equipment does a high-caliber swimmer use to prepare for competition?

SWIMMING GOGGLES

What makes a good pair of swimming goggles? Many swimmers spend years looking for the perfect pair while others never seem to. Some send away to exotic countries for kits to make their own eyewear and some just make do with whatever they can find at the local sporting good store. I'm going to save you a lot of time and effort and share a secret.

Your FACE makes good goggles.

No I'm not trying to be flippant. I'm just laying out a very simple and straightforward fact. Your facial structure determines which kind of swimming goggles will fit and work for you best, specifically, the topography of your temples, eyes, brow, and bridge of the nose. So before you go off the sporting-goods store to buy a broad range of goggles in the hopes of finding one that works, take an honest appraisal of your face in the mirror. If you have an aquiline nose, a pronounced eyebrow ridge, deep set eyes, or pronounced cheekbones, the smaller box-like goggles are probably for you. The smallest of which were once only sold via mail order from Sweden. Now you can get them online – try Swim Outlet, or google "Swedish swim goggles." They still usually arrive in a kit and you will have to supply your own string for the nose piece. However, if you have a flatter face, a wider or smaller nose, or wide set eyes, the bug-eye goggles might be for you. (Bug-eye goggles always fit me best and my favorite style was made by Tyr.) An honest self-appraisal will get you on the path to finding a perfect fit, but now that we've determined which type of swimming goggles will work for you best, it's time to explore.

Go to a few sporting-goods stores in your area and sit yourself down in the swimming accessories section. Start trying on goggles. Many sporting-goods stores are used to swimmers going through their swimming gear so if you're clean and put them back in the packaging the way they were when you took them out, they usually won't mind you trying on as many pairs as you need. Place the goggles over your eyes and pull the strap over your head. Once the strap is set, press them onto your eyes with the heels of your hands. The seal should contact your skin the entire way around and you should feel your eyeballs sucked slightly into the goggles. If you feel air near your eyes, or if you feel gaps in the seal, try another pair.

Next, you'll want to test them to see if they'll stay on during a dive. Few sporting-goods stores, if any, have their own swimming pools in them so here's a trick I learned to test the seal. Once you've got these goggles set on your eyes, take your fingertips and tug, lightly, on the top rims of the goggles just under your eyebrows. If the seal breaks, they will never survive a dive into the water and you should keep looking for another pair. If the seal does not break, you've got yourself a good pair of swimming goggles. Buy this pair and go try them in the pool.

Once you have a pair of goggles you love to death are you done looking for goggles? No. Goggles, like all equipment, wear out. So once you do find that perfect pair, save up your money and buy out the stores in your area. Swimming goods manufacturers love to think that goggles are fashionable. As such, they love to create new designs every few years. I can't count the number of times my friends and I would have a set of goggles falling off our faces because our beloved designs were no longer made. Do not let this happen to you. Getting a stash of good goggles allows you to last out the fashion cycle to a time when they'll be "hip" to making your style of goggles again.

SWIMMING CAPS

After goggles, swimming caps are the most common optional piece of gear in the sport. The commonly held belief is that the latex or rubber cap provides less drag through the water than flowing hair, and that a cap will protect the hair from the caustic chemicals in most swimming pools. Not true. The truth about swimming caps is they're hot, hot, HOT. This is why most swimmers don't use them in practice and only female swimmers or swimmers with long hair commonly wear them. So let's look at the swimming cap's perceived benefits and decide whether the use of one is really for you.

Performance

Swimming caps make you faster, right? Nope. The difference in drag between a closely cropped head of hair and a cap is minimal at best. Furthermore, that cap acts like an insulator keeping all the heat your head is trying to radiate away from your body, while highly exerting yourself, trapped. Most of a body's working fatigue comes from the heat generated by the muscles in the act of working. When the muscle gets hot, it becomes ineffective. The body tries to cool muscles by moving more blood through them and by increasing skin evaporation rates by sweating. The blood is moved towards the skin where evaporation can help cool the body and the working muscles down. One of the primary areas where the body tries to evaporate excess heat is the head, which is why your face gets red if you're working out. Insulating your head while working hard stops your body from being able to cool down and results in faster and deeper fatigue. So if this is the case, why are caps used at all?

The drawbacks to swimming with a cap on are cumulative. So over a short period of time, say that of a 50, the swimmer will hardly notice any increase in fatigue. However, once a swimmer is exerting themselves for longer distances, say 200 and higher, the difference in fatigue becomes noticeable. You will often see many distance swimmers eschewing the use of a cap in order to stave off heat-based fatigue as long as possible. The only time that a swimming cap is really useful is if you have long hair.

If you have hair that gets in your eyes or even your mouth when you're trying to breathe, then a cap is really necessary. Turning or moving your head in order to get the hair out of your way can alter your stroke drastically, ruining your body position and resulting in slower times. So for swimmers who swim shorter races but have longer hair, the cap isn't a bad idea. But, a swimming cap will help protect my hair, right? Sorry.

Hair Care

A swimming cap has not yet been invented to keep the caustic water of a swimming pool away from your hair. Caps are also made out of materials that themselves are damaging to hair. The latex or silicone pulls, breaks, and splits hair in ways only the Marquis de Sade would find appealing. Furthermore, the water that does get into a cap has a chance to really soak those chemicals deep into your hair and ruin your hair that way. If you really care about your hair (though you might guess that most swimmers just give up), you will need to treat it every time you finish your practice.

Once you get out of the water, and have taken care of your swimsuit, take a shower. Wash the hair with shampoo, and rinse it out completely. The water from the shower is normal tap water and thus nowhere near as caustic to your hair as the pool water you just left. Washing your hair will remove all the chemicals that swimming in the pool put in. Next, and most importantly, apply conditioner. The chemicals in pool water have, during your practice, settled on the hair follicles and leached them of all the natural oils that keep it safe from breaking. Conditioner will return as much of that oil to your hair as you need. Specialty hair products have recently been invented to prevent severe damage to the hair follicles.

Cap Use

If you must keep your golden locks intact and have figured out how to maintain that gorgeous mane of yours with shampoo and conditioner, how on earth do you get a cap on your head? Well believe it or not, before I figured out that a cap was not for me, I developed a way of putting a cap on that worked well for me. Now I've seen many swimmers put a cap on wet. They fill the cap with water, bend at the waist, and displace the water in the cap with their head. This sets the cap nicely on your head, but as soon as you dive in the water, the wet hair inside the cap acts like a lubricant and can shift the cap over your goggles or even back over your head to get caught in the goggle strap. Not only are you without your cap, but you're also swimming blind.

To combat the shifting of the cap during the dive, many of us developed a method of putting on the cap dry. Be sure if you have long hair, that you've braided, pinned, or bunned (whatever it is you do to get your hair up and out of the way) prior to this process or you will rip it out of your head. Arrange the cap so that you are holding onto the sides with the cap upside down and the front "brim" facing your chest. Take that brim and place it firmly at your forehead. While tilting your head forward, pull your hands, which are still holding the sides of the cap, down to your shoulders. This seats the cap firmly across the front and top of your head. Then slowly return the sides of the cap to behind your ears. At this point you can tuck in any stray hair that might have come loose during the process. If done right it looks like you're the Incredible Hulk bursting out of your cap and can be very intimidating to your opponents. Furthermore, the dry hair and skin under the cap act like a seal against water coming in under the cap and making it mobile. Water will still seep in, but it will happen slowly, allowing your dive to be unaffected by equipment malfunctions.

I know this is all pretty daunting which is why swimmers the world over keep rediscovering the following truth: the best thing you can do for your hair and for your performance is to cut it off. Nothing ever beats a shaved head in the water and nothing protects your hair like no hair.

SWIMSUITS

Swimsuits are the one piece of required equipment to a swimmer. Caps, goggles, and nose plugs, however useful they are, can't match the vital importance of a suit.

So what makes a good suit? I won't go into the details of the latest full-body suits benefits and drawbacks here since far too much has been said on their behalf, but if you want to read my thoughts on this "innovation," please consult my section on performance enhancement. The best swimsuits fit snugly without restricting movement or blood flow. For men, take the size of your tightest blue jeans, and drop two inches off the size. For women, or if you're braving a full-body suit, pick a suit that covers your chest snugly. A loose suit will scoop water, and no one swims very fast when they're carrying around a few extra gallons.

I got an up-close and personal example of the dangers of women's suit scooping when I was at one of the US Swimming's training events. Several of us guys thought it would be funny to do a relay at the end of the day wearing women's suits. Each of us borrowed one of our female teammates' training suits in order to be properly costumed for the event. Now, unlike competition suits, training suits are either bought to just cover the body or are competition suits that have worn out. Either way, these suits are very loose. So having donned these suits and enjoyed the joke as we headed to the starting blocks with our borrowed attire I prepared to dive in for my length of the relay. As soon as I dove in I knew something was wrong.

The chest of the suit, being used to holding the very well proportioned body of the swimmer I had borrowed it from, expanded to its accustomed size and dragged me straight to the bottom of the pool. Frantically I tried to correct my course, but it was too late. Stars filled my vision as my head contacted with the bottom of the pool. Dazed and confused, I regained my body position and began to swim the relay again with this anchor around my chest. As I hit the turn the suit once again tried to drag me to the bottom but I was able to correct this time and finish the race. I found a deep respect for female swimmers that day.

Now if not kept snug and new, the full-body suits will do exactly the same thing. So how do I take care of my competition suit so it lasts? Well eventually all suits loosen and wear out. At best you can extend their useful competition life but that's about it. Every time you leave the pool, make sure you rinse the suit out in cold water. This action gets rid of the high chemical content water which breaks down the fibers in the swimsuit. Next squeeze the excess water out of the suit, don't wring them out excessively. Then, air-dry the suit. Blow drying a swimsuit with a hot hair dryer, or using one of those suit centrifuges will also break down the fibers. Broken fibers lead to stretching and eventually, sagging and drag.

Once your competition suit has loosened, it's time to use it to replace your workout suit, which probably has holes in it anyway.

TOWELS

Every swimmer needs a towel. It keeps you warm, it dries you off, it's your bed and in a pinch, it's your private room. When the locker room is not available, you can use it to change into (or out of) your suit and when you're hiding from your coach, it can be your refuge. A towel is so many things to a competitive swimmer, but what makes a good one? Swimmers use towels for so many varied jobs that it needs to be pretty large to do its myriad of tasks. Ideally the towel should be between 7 and 8 feet long and 3 to 4 feet wide for adult swimmers and correspondingly smaller for younger ones. You want to be able to lay comfortably on it with your head on your swimming bag. You also want it to be able to circle your body twice if you're using it as a surrogate locker room. Never seen this done? Sure you have. Watch for any male swimmer who has a towel wrapped around his body but higher than his waist. You'll see him kick off his suit and put on his pants while never leaving modesty behind.

The primary job of a towel, though, is to dry you off. Since a swimmer is in and out of the water so many times during a meet, the best towels for this job are double thick. One side of the towel is terrycloth while the other is a shammy. Not only is this a more absorbent towel, but it's also very warm. Simple terrycloth towels get damp far too quickly and then are pretty well useless. Shammys can be very absorbent but there's a reason only divers use them. A shammy has to stay damp in order to absorb water so they dry but not completely. Now divers, who are in and out of the water even more than swimmers use these little things between dives during competition, but once they're done, they use a towel like the rest of us.

When you're looking for a new towel, be sure to get a dark colored one. This towel will go from locker room to locker room, to your car, to the swimming pool deck many times before it completely frays into oblivion. If you get a white towel you'll end up bleaching it to death in order to make it look passable and all that washing will leave it less absorbent anyway.

So when you're looking for a good towel, get a dark colored, thick, big towel. Most stores call these beach towels, but be careful you get one that's thick enough. Most beach towels are only terry cloth and meant to keep the sand off beach combers toes. You need one that will stand up to the wear of years of practicing, meets, and other abuse. Good towels are expensive, but a necessary part of a swimmer's equipment. So how do you take care of a good towel?

Always lay out your towel to dry after each time using it. Never ball it up and use it for a pillow. That's what your clothes in your swimming bag are for. If you're between practices, lay it out in the back seat of your car. When you can, lay it out over an outdoor fence on sunny days to let it air out. When you must wash your towel, wash it on delicate cycle with fabric softener and definitely no bleach. This way your favorite towel will be at your side for many years to come.

EVENT PREPARATION

You've done your training. You've honed your technique. Now it's time to put it all on the line and race. But what do the top competitive swimmers do get ready for race-day? Well if you treated the meet like any normal day of exercise you wouldn't do very well. Competitive swimmers do a number of things to make sure they're ready to perform their best. They taper their workouts, shave, change their nutritional regimen, get lots of rest, and calm their minds before the big day. In this section we'll discuss how the best swimmers in the world get ready for the championship races.

EVENT WARMUP

While warming up is an integral part of your every day workout schedule, on the day of your meet, your event warm up takes on special significance. If you don't do it well on any regular day, there's no problem, you can just adapt the next stage of your workout to recover. If you warm up poorly on race day? You've just blown six to twelve months of work. There's a lot of pressure there, I know. It makes a person not want to get out of bed on event-day, but cheer up. Competitive swimmers have been tackling this high-pressure situation for many years and survived. You can too. Here's how it's done.

Most swim meets are day-long affairs, starting in the wee hours of the morning and lasting until well after sundown. The warm up time for events like these usually starts around 7:00 AM and goes to around 9:00 AM. Everyone who has qualified for this meet and has an event today will be in the pool trying to get warmed up now. The pool will be very crowded. If you're one of those swimmers who likes to have a lane to themselves when they workout, get over it fast. In all likelihood you'll have the feet of one swimmer in your face while you feel your toes being tickled by the swimmer behind you. Don't be intimidated by the number of bodies in the pool, just get your distance in and move on to the next phase of the warm up.

How far do you need to go to be properly warmed up for your event? That distance will vary depending up on the swimmer. If your daily workout is somewhere near 1-2k, you'll really only need a 200 or so to get warmed up. If your daily workout is near 20k, it will be closer to 1.5k. Just do the distance at an easy but strong pace. What does this mean? When I say, "easy" that means don't go balls-to-the-wall fast. That's a recipe for pulled muscles and disaster. Don't go slow either, though. By "strong" I mean that you should be able to feel the water resist you as you pull and against your feet. Stress your muscles just enough that you get some power from your strokes and kick. Once you feel your body able to smoothly accept your commands for power and efficiency that you've trained all year to instill into your muscle-memory, you're done and ready to move onto the next phase of warm up.

Now if warming up our muscles was all there was to getting ready for your event, we'd be done. However, every pool, and every year of preparation is different and you'll need to test your body and its interaction with the pool at speed in order to be truly prepared for your event. Towards the last 30 minutes of the warm up time, swimmers and coaches will gather at the lanes at the sides of the pool in order to do this last bit of preparation. Sprinters practice their starts, do a 25, and into one flip turn. Think of this like the drag racers practicing at the starting line before their race. They're testing their machines and how they react to the track. This is exactly what you're doing. You've done up to a year of training to get to this point so your body will be different from the last time you did this. Feel how the pool reacts to the power that you put into it. Is the variation in water temperature different form your workout pool making the water feel different? Is the variation in the depth of the pool causing an interference with your stroke as you ride over it? How does the wall design and markings affect your approach to your turn? As a sprinter, you only get one chance at these obstacles in your race so you'd better find out now how they affect your stroke.

If you're a distance swimmer, do some 50s at your race pace. Feel how well the lane lines impede the wave action from the other lanes. If they don't, drafting will be very easy. Adjust your strategy accordingly. Find out the most efficient way to approach and attack the walls for your flip turns. Adjust your timing to the wall to adjust to differences to your workout pool. If there are depth variances in this pool, get a feel for how you're going to react to them proactively and not let them slow you down. This is your time to make sure that you understand this pool as well as you can before you have to put it all on the line in a race. Make it count.

Now if your event is close to the warm up time, you're ready to go. However, as we all know, swim meets are many-hour long affairs. After two hours or so of staying warm and loose, even the best of warm-ups starts to wear off. So how can we make sure that your body is warmed up and ready for your race even if it's six hours after the warm-ups? Well for higher-end competitions, that's not a problem. The pool complexes used for these events have several pools available to competitors and as such, around an hour before your event is scheduled, you can warm up in this pool to keep your body ready for your race. In other swimming meets held at facilities that have only one pool, you have to be creative.

When you feel your warmed up body start to get stale during the day, you're going to need to warm your body up again a bit in order to stay at peak readiness. In my days of swimming meets, I've tried calisthenics, isometrics, and even warm showers to stay warm. Calisthenics can be useful in order to get the heart-rate up but you need to be careful that you don't jar joints or over do. Ten jumping jacks, pushups, or sit ups will usually work. Isometrics can be used to since they're a lot easier on the joints. You can mimic your stroke with one hand and create slight resistance with the other to stay warmed up. A warm shower can even work as long as you don't let your body get too hot or cold since both will sap your energy.

When you approach your race you want to feel that your body is as ready as it can be for the trial ahead. You've worked and trained your body for up to a year and you have fine tuned yourself with an excellent warm up. Now it's time to see what you can do.

RACE DAY NUTRITION

There are many guides out there that tell you what you should be eating in order to build muscle mass or have a high level of energy during your workouts, but when it comes to the day of the race, should you really be eating the same things? Not really. Once race day is here, your body is prepared, trained, and fueled up just about as much as it's going to be. Nutrition on the day of your race is primarily about not screwing up what you've worked so long to achieve. Some nutrition "experts" say that you need to carbo-load the day before the race, but since the storage of energy reserves in your muscles is done days ahead of time by your body, carbo loading really only should be done the week before your race. Stuffing your body with too much complex carbohydrates and proteins is a sure way to make you sluggish for your event-day races. So carbo load early. About a week before the race, increase your intake of complex carbohydrates like pastas, baked potatoes, rice, and beans. Don't worry too much about the fat and oil content of the food this early out. Your body will know what to do with them before race day and any deleterious effects the food will have on your body will be over by the day of your race. On the day of the race, though, you have to be more careful.

One of the mistakes many athletes make is over-hydration. Nutritionists, and coaches the world over have been telling athletes to keep drinking until you need to urinate during your events to avoid dehydration. While dehydration has a terrible effect on an athlete's effectiveness, over-hydration can be just as bad. Water, by its nature is great at carrying other substances into our bodies, but when you over-hydrate, all those wonderful vitamins, proteins, and minerals that you worked so hard to put in your body are carried away by all that water you're passing through your body and into the toilet. A simple rule of thumb is, if you have to urinate more than once every two hours, you're over hydrated and losing effectiveness. Just cut back a little on the water and you'll be fine.

Another mistake many athletes make is to fill up on food before the race, assuming that they'll need the fuel to perform at their peak. The fact is, that while a pancake and egg breakfast is enjoyable, it's hardly the kind of food you need to be carrying around with you while you try to beat your best time. Complex carbohydrates and proteins take a long time to digest and the energy your body is using to digest that food can better be used in making you go faster. Smaller breakfasts are usually preferable since they provide the body with less to work on during your event. One bowl of oatmeal and a piece of fruit is probably the best choice you can make for race day fodder. If you really need to pound the carbs, though, do it at dinner, at night between race days that way your body will have time to digest all those carbs and put them to good use.

Energy drinks are another commonly misused nutritional item in the athlete's arsenal. Many commercials selling these drinks show athletes chugging these elixirs with reckless abandon as they jump around in their sport. In reality you really don't want to have more than a sip of this stuff at a time. These drinks are filled with salts, minerals, sugars, and other carbs that may make you have a sugar crash minutes after drinking them. Furthermore, as your body metabolizes these salts and sugars, it uses more water to put them to use which may end up dehydrating you. If you feel you must drink these things, water them down a lot. Then you can be sure you're not using up more liquid than you're ingesting in the process of drinking.

I can hear some of you saying, "you've told us what not to do, what can we eat and drink on race day?" Well every body's different and every athlete needs to learn to listen to what their body is telling them on race day. What worked for me may not work for you so listen to your body. If you have a sudden craving for something, listen to it. That's your body telling you something is needed. Now I'm not saying that you should give in as soon as you have the munchies for a candy bar, but if you have a hankering for something sweet, get a banana, apple, or some other piece of fruit. On the other hand, if you feel you need something salty, don't go straight for the chips, take a sip of an energy drink (there's more salt in those things than you know).

When I was racing at my peak ability, my morning meal consisted of a banana and a small bowl of oatmeal. During the day of the race, if I got hungry again, I'd sneak a bagel (though by the vagaries of the race day, I rarely was hungry until after the day's races were done). Once I got back to the hotel from the day of races, I'd hit the local Italian restaurant for a bowl of pasta (a good fettuccini alfredo was my favorite). Though, if I had finals that night, I'd eat something smaller like a bowl of soup and carbo load after finals.

I said it earlier, and I'll say it again, though. Every athlete is different. Your body knows what it needs at every stage of your training development, tapir, and race-day. Once you learn to listen to it and give your body what it needs, you'll be on your way to some spectacular results.

SHAVING

Yes, Virginia, male swimmers shave their legs. Now that we have that titillation out of the way we can be more accurate. Not only do swimmers shave their legs, but they shave their arms, chest, back, neck, face, and sometimes their head. Anything not covered by underwear is fair game. So why do swimmers shave? When shaving was originally explained to me, I was told that my body hair created a significant amount of drag in the water and removing that hair would make me faster. Now the fact that I was prepubescent at the time and had less hair on my body than a peach was immaterial. I laid out the money for my first razor and can of shaving cream. We had a party in one of my teammate's hotel rooms and shaved on towels, using empty wastepaper baskets as buckets, while we watched music videos. The first thing I noticed when I was done with my first shave was how cold I was.

Meteorologists use the term wind-chill in order to describe when the human body's warm air pocket is assaulted by cold air, making the air seem colder than it actually is. When a person shaves, they remove the little bit of hair and dead skin that helps maintain that protective barrier of warm air around our bodies. When a swimmer shaves they take off as much skin and hair as possible because heat exchange, not drag reduction, is the swimmer's primary goal in this activity.

Somewhere near 80% of a muscle's fatigue is caused by the heat generated in the act of working. When a muscle overheats the body tries to cool it down by sweating, moving more blood through the muscle, and breathing harder.

Swimmers, luckily, swim in their own radiator. They swim in pools. Competition pools are even kept two or three degrees colder than other pools in order to help swimmers stave off this heat-related fatigue. When a swimmer shaves, they enhance their rate of heat-exchange with the water immensely by removing as much of the body's insulation that they can get away with.

When it comes to shaving, swimmers have more in common with Sweeney Todd than Sandra Dee. They both go after their chore with a reckless abandon, cackling at their bloody work. Swimmers consider it a badge of honor to enter a meet with at least a few battle scars. Typical places for you to slice yourself up are at the ankles, the fronts and back of the knees, the elbows, the base of the sides of the neck, the inner groin, and around the nipples. The skin is not very smooth around these areas since it does a lot of stretching and contracting in normal movement. So if you want to be gentle, these are the places to be careful. Even nipples will grow back if sliced off, but it's not pleasant.

So now that we've established that this is no mere hair removal and exfoliation, let's get down to the business of telling you how the this ritual is done. You'll need a good set of electric clippers; Wahl makes the best I have seen in my opinion. You will also need a large package of razors and a can of moisturizing shaving cream, and lots and lots of warm water. First use the clippers to remove all hair on your body not covered by a swimming suit. Whether you decide to leave hair on your head is a personal choice, but if you are leaving hair there, get a short haircut before the race-day. This hair that the clippers removes helps the next stage of the operation since it's coarse and quickly clogs any razor making it ineffective at exfoliation. You want to save the sharpness of your razors for slicing off as much dead skin as you can.

Next, you'll want to take a hot shower. If you're in a hotel room, as most of us are before a big event, leave the bathroom door open so that the steam fills the room. Skin and hair both become much more manageable once they've been in a moist environment. The shower will also wash off all the hair from your clipping that could get in the way of your blade. Once your shower is done, fill a bucket (most of us use an empty wastepaper basket or an ice bucket that most hotels provide) with very warm to almost hot water. Put a towel on the floor where you plan to do your work so as to not leave a big mess for the hotel maids and stand or sit on it. Wet down the area of skin you plan to shave with water from the bucket and ready your shaving cream.

Having shaved for races a number of times, I eventually settled on Edge Foaming Gel as my preferred shaving cream. Its moisturizers, which are designed for the delicate skin of the face, really help the thin skin that you leave yourself with after this ritual. Edge, unlike some less expensive shaving cream must be worked after squirting it, so once you have a quarter-sized dollop on your hand rub it into the area you plan to shave. You will find that it expands a lot and covers more than you thought it would. Once you have the shaving cream worked into your skin, ready your razor.

What razor is best for swimmers? Unfortunately the multi-blade razors that are all the rage these days are not ideal. The small spaces between the blades easily clog with skin and hair. The more spaces that can clog, the faster the whole razor becomes ineffectual. In my opinion, the best razor for swimmers is a simple one-bladed razor. It can be cleared easily and once it's dull, you can throw it away and start with the next one in the package (make sure you buy 10 or so to always have a sharp razor available). Now most people who shave for vanity do a very light pass of the razor over the skin with the grain of the hair. This just won't work for a swimmer. Start at the bottom of the grain, the direction in which all the hair is growing, and shave against the grain using as much force as comfortable. Once you've made a six to eight inch pass, push the razor against the skin in the opposite direction back to where you started. This back and forth action shaves off dead skin then clears it from the razor on the return path. You will need to perform this action several times in order to shave thoroughly enough to receive a benefit from the shaving ritual.

How many times should I do this back and forth with the razor? That's different for different people and will become necessarily more as you age and your body gets used to this ritual. Once you think an area of skin has been shaved enough, bring the skin next to a bare light bulb. If you see anything sticking up from your skin at all, it's time to lather up and go again. If not, you've done well. You will know you've shaved an area of skin too much when you see mottled flecks of red well up on the skin. That means you've cut through all the dead skin on that part of the body and are down to new, living skin that still gets blood from your body.

Once you've finished to your satisfaction, you'll want to moisturize your remaining skin. Again, I find myself preferring another men's shaving aid. Nivea makes a quality moisturizing product which, through being designed for the face, works very well for a swimmer's razor-scoured skin. Once you've moisturized yourself, it will probably be time to administer first-aid.

Razor cuts bleed. There's no two ways around it. And swimmers cut themselves a lot. Since the cuts are done with a very sharp instrument you won't clot anywhere near as fast as with a common abrasion. On the bright side, though, they tend to heal fast since the instrument that caused the injury is likely very sharp and quite clean. I've found that simple pressure with a clean towel or tissue paper, if necessary, works very well for cuts around the problem areas of your body. Just apply pressure for about a minute and you'll have the makings of a new battle scar story. The cut will probably sting a bit when you get in the water the first time but after that, you'll be used to it.

Now that you're fully shaved you will probably feel very cold. Get in your warmest sweats, climb into bed, and watch some TV.

CONDITIONING

The conditioning of swimmers is the best of all athletes in the world. Why? Because the nature of their sport is so physically demanding that anything less makes performance of their events a physical impossibility. Weightlifters, boxers, and football players are all trained to push their bodies for short bursts of energy over a long period of time and while their bodies take a pounding, swimmers never get these rests. When a swimmer puts forth a burst of energy, it has to come on top of the energy that is already being expended in simply continuing to move forward in the pool. You might argue that this energy requirement is a lot like running, but a runner needn't expend energy to simply stand still. The water is constantly leeching heat and energy from a swimmer's body and the act of staying still in the water, requires that a swimmer float, requiring more concentration and energy than simply sitting still on land.

A swimmer, furthermore, lives in a world of almost constant resistance in the water. Every action is resisted a little bit by the water in which he swims. Thus, unlike weightlifting, swimming constantly works muscle groups that are just impossible to isolate properly with free-weights or weight machines. A swimmer in training will burn through millions of calories in a day and still be starving for more because of this resistance. Furthermore, since there is such a small amount of physical pounding that a swimmer must endure; swimmers will practice for hours and hours in order to be in good enough shape for their competitions.

In this section I'll discuss how the best swimmers in the world train for their events and what they do for those four to six hours each day while they're training. I'll also post some of the workouts we used to do so you can use them for your own benefit as you work your way through the process of training to be a swimmer. Swimmers aren't a terribly dainty crew, so this section isn't for the faint-hearted, but if you want to become a good swimmer, here's where to start.

WARM UP

If practice is a smorgasbord, the warm up is your appetizer. Starting with stretching, before you even get in the water, the warm up phase of your workout should take between ten and twenty-five percent of your workout time and distance. Many young-guns out there don't pay attention to the warming up because they feel like they get their bodies ready in the first minute or two of practice. This is only completely true if you're only doing 1000 in your entire workout. However, if you're going to be swimming for several miles during your workout, even the youngest swimmer will need a good warm up.

Everyone starts practice with stretching, and if you don't, you really should. Stretching lets the body know that physical exertion will soon be required of it. Each stretch resets the muscle in a state ready for action from a resting state where it may have built up fluids from sitting at a desk all day. Some people believe that a bouncing stretch works best for waking up a muscle, but I find that stresses the muscles, ligaments, and tendons more than is needed. Simply bring your muscle to a stretch where it starts to be painful, hold it for ten seconds, then gradually let go. For the quads, pull your ankle up to your buttocks. For your triceps, put your hand on the back of your neck with your elbow up in the air. Take your other hand and pull on that elbow in a line across the top of your shoulders. For your calves, find a wall and lean on it while keeping your heels on the ground. Lower yourself towards the wall until you feel a good stretch, hold for those ten seconds, then release slowly. In a similar fashion, stretch out your forearms, hamstrings, lats, and pectorals. You may feel it necessary to have a partner stretch you but I strongly recommend against it. The other person has no idea what you're feeling and will often overstretch your body in ways that may damage it. Better to break the stretch up into manageable bits and use a wall where you are in complete control of the stretch. For instance, if you are stretching your pectoral muscles, use a wall by putting your palm on the wall at shoulder height, and turning your body until you feel the proper stretch. Once you are done, do the other side. Now that you're done stretching, it's time to get in the water.

Some swimmers prefer to get into the water slowly to keep their bodies loose. I've never noticed a difference in warm up effectiveness between getting in fast or slow, so I usually just dive in. Now, if you're young and impetuous, and I once was, you'll want to start swimming at top speed right away. Unfortunately, even though you feel fine, your body really isn't up to working at peak efficiency right away. Now, if you've had a hard workout the day before, and are still stiff from the previous exercise, you'll feel more of a need for a warm up. A good warm up will take your body from the stretched out state you left it in outside the pool, to a state where you can push your body to the limit, no matter what shape you started practice in.

Start by diving in and focusing intently on your stroke. You should feel the water as closely as you can while you catch, pull, and release the water. The stiffness from yesterday's workouts and from sitting at a desk all day at school should slowly leave your muscles as you clear your first 200 or so of your warm up. Once you're past this milestone, you will want to ramp up your effort so that by the end of the warm up your heart rate is somewhere near 120 beats per minute (bpm). By warming up gradually, you have brought your muscles ready to work at peak efficiency, you have gradually brought your tendons and ligaments into readiness by stressing them slightly, and you have brought your heart and lungs into readiness by letting them get used to the work they're going to need to do to support your body through the upcoming workout.

When I warm up, it generally takes me a few lengths to return my body to the feel for the water that I'm used to when I'm practicing. To start it feels like my body has that same feeling that you do when you wake up from a deep sleep and you can't close your hands all the way. Only in this case, I feel that way all over my body. Gradually as I warm up, that feeling of detachment goes away and I can interact fully with the water, as I know I should. It is no lie to say that a good warm up forestalls injury. Each part of your body that you take care of during warm up has one less reason to fail and injure you than it did before getting it ready. Warmed up muscles, don't pull and warmed up tendons don't fray (and create tendonitis). You're doing yourself a big, long-term favor by warming up well. Never abandon that advantage.

WEIGHTS

Every sport these days has an associated strength program, but swimmers use weights in a very specific manner. A swimmer's body needs to be flexible and quick. As such, a strength program that bulks up a body at the expense of endurance, speed, and flexibility is counterproductive at best. So when Mr. Lars MuscleBound takes you through your first gym workout, smile and nod, and do what he says. What he's just shown you will be the perfect method of strength training for almost any sport but swimming. He'll have you using your full range of motion, isolating the proper muscle groups, and performing your reps very slowly in order to get the most out of your workout. That's great for the run-of-the-mill athlete, but you're a swimmer. You need to do something different.

Control the Weight

Whether you're doing free-weights or machines, the same thing holds true for swimming strength training. Speed and flexibility are key. You work on your endurance in the water so nothing you do while strength training will hold a candle to what you do in the pool. Your heart rate in the gym won't ever go above 120 bpm when you're in shape. So you're only in the gym to work on your strength and speed. Here's how it's done.

Each time you take a rep in a strength workout you will want to explode up with the weight and bring it down as slowly as you can. Now some swimmers when they first start this method of strength training throw the weight around, but this isn't what you want to do. You want to push up as fast as you can without losing control. You know you've lost control when the weight bounces at the top of the rep cycle. Never let it bounce. You can injure yourself if you do, and torn muscles (and worse) are not fun. What I do when I'm strength training is count the rep number as I explode up while keeping under control, then I count 2, 3, 4, on the way down as slowly as I possibly can. This way you work on your explosiveness on the way up, and your flexibility on the way down.

As a swimmer, you'll also want to do more reps than the average athlete does. You're not looking to stack the machine or lift the biggest barbell in the gym. As a swimmer, you're looking to push your muscle groups to failure at the end of every set. Your first set at a machine or a particular muscle group should go for around 12 to 20 reps before failure. Your next set at the same machine (with 10% more weight) should go from 8 to 12 reps before failure, and your third set (with 20% more) should go from 6 to 8 reps before failure. This way you've pushed every range of motion within your isolated muscle group to its limit and broken it down so it can be built back stronger as you rest and recover.

Remember though, that most people are in the gym in order to get in shape and when you do several sets at one machine or on one set of free-weights, you'll want to let them work through between your sets. Doing so, gives you just the right amount of rest between sets and keeps good old Lars happy since you're not pissing off his customers by "hogging" the machines.

INJURIES AND AILMENTS

One might think that in the neutral environment of a swimming pool, it would be a very stupid or unlucky swimmer that became injured. Quite the contrary. Swimmers by the nature of their sport, and the environment in which their sport must take place, are prone to a very specific group of injuries and ailments that are so common that the medical community has named some after the sport itself. In this section I'll try to describe common ailments that swimmers encounter in the course of their everyday training, competing, and in the act of just being around pools so much.

SWIMMER'S EAR

Sometimes the most insidious ailments come with the most innocuous names: Swimmer's Ear. Sounds like some kid just got in the pool for the first time and is whining that the water won't come out of his ears. In reality swimmer's ear is a chronic and sometimes debilitating condition that affects swimmers the world over. It's so common that the FDA has recently been considering adding a swimmer's ear inoculation to its list of recommended shots to protect the hearing of children under the age of twelve. What's unfortunate is a very simple preventative measure keeps swimmer's ear at bay. It's cheap, easy to administer, and very safe.

Before I get to the remedy though, let's talk about the symptoms. Swimmer's ear usually starts with an itch deep in the ear canal. When you see someone at the pool with a finger in their ear wiggling it up and down rapidly, you know they've got it. The next stage of swimmer's ear is pain. Any time you touch the ear around the canal or the ear cartilage connected to the ear canal, you will feel a sharp stab of pain shooting from your ear to your throat behind your jaw. If left untreated at this point, your ear may swell up enough so you cannot close your mouth and you're risking damage to your middle or even inner ear. Sounds pretty nasty eh? Well there's an easy fix.

Vinegar.

That's right, all the doctor's visits, all the penicillin, inoculations, creams, and ointments can't do what this over the counter remedy does. A simple vinegar and water solution mixed in equal parts kills the bacteria that cause swimmer's ear and it costs less than a penny per application. So buy an empty eyedropper bottle and fill it one half of the way with white vinegar and the other half with tap water and keep it in your swimming bag. Every time you finish practicing use the eyedropper to put 3 or 4 drops of the vinegar solution in your ear and wait 30 seconds. Do the same then to the other ear. This remedy may make you smell like a salad, but it will take care of any minor case of swimmer's ear in a few weeks. Furthermore, as a preventative measure, the vinegar solution is ideal for those of us who are prone to swimmer's ear. However, if your case of swimmer's ear is advanced, you should of course, see your doctor.

FUNGAL INFECTIONS

Trench foot, crotch rot, athlete's foot, and some more derogatory terms all apply to problems that affect all swimmers at one point in their careers: fungal infections. Swimmers spend most of their lives in dank, dark, moist environments, especially when you're in a pool for 5 to 6 hours a day, getting dressed in a pool locker room before and after practice and end up with a wet head for an hour or so after that. As any jungle explorer will tell you, that's just asking for trouble.

As with most health problems, the best thing a swimmer can do is take preventative measures against the single-celled onslaught. Here are some tips that have worked for me.

Don't wear your damp swimsuit home under your clothing. Many swimmers at some time in their careers need to get to another event after swimming quickly. They've somehow forgotten underwear or have worn their suit under their clothing in order to save time before practice. Fungus loves dark, wet, warm places to grow and if you have a wet swimsuit on under warm clothing, that's just asking for an infection. Even if it feels a bit strange, it's still better to go commando if you have no (or wet) underwear. This way you're warm and dry and safe from rot.

Dry out your swimsuit and towel completely between practices. Fungus spores are remarkably resilient so the drier your equipment stays, the safer your skin will be. Now I know that it is difficult to keep your suit and towel dry when you're going from morning practice to school, to evening practice. The cloth only really has seven or eight hours to dry while you're at school, but every little bit helps. Hang up your suit in your locker or even in your car, and do the same with your towel. It may look strange, but we never joined swimming to be "normal" did we?

Dry off completely before getting into your clothing. I know you're going to be in a hurry to get home to eat or to get to school, or whatever other practice you're shoehorning into your day, but not using your time in the locker room to dry off completely is asking for trouble. You'll want to towel off from the top to the bottom, starting at your head and hair then your arms, back, chest, suit-area, legs and feet. This way no water drips down as you're trying to dry yourself. Once you're done, get dressed from the top down. That way the parts of your body that aren't fully dry will have time to do so as you clothe yourself.

Hang your goggles out to dry completely between practices. You'd be surprised at how many eye infections start with damp goggles. Just like your suit and towel, make sure you hang out your goggles to dry between practices. I usually hung mine from my rear-view mirror in the car.

Find a dry place to put your socks and shoes back on after practices. Since feet usually go inside socks then shoes, they need special care to make sure they stay dry as you're getting dressed. Find a dry spot on the floor, and dry off your feet, especially between the toes. Then put a sock and shoe on one foot then a sock and shoe on the other. If you cannot find a dry spot, place your shoes on the floor and put your feet on top of your shoes as you dry your feet.

If, for whatever reason, you haven't been able to take these precautions, the first sign that you might have a fungal infection is itchy skin in the affected area. As soon as this happens you will probably want to invest in a cure of some sort.

The most common areas for swimmers to get fungal infections are the feet, between the legs, under the armpits, and around the eyes. Most athletes foot remedies will handle any problems with your feet, but other, more delicate areas of your body will need a different remedy. For between the legs and in the armpits, most jock itch remedies will do the trick. For infections around the eyes though, you will have to be very careful not to get the fungicide in your eyes.

If a fungal infection is allowed to progress, though, the affected skin will peel and become red and tender to the touch. It will, however, still itch. Infections around the eye generally just show as flaky skin patches. For the most part none of these health issues are really life-altering. They are annoying and if they become visible, they can be embarrassing, so keep dry when you can.

TENDONITIS

Aside from swimmer's ear, tendonitis is the most common swimmer's injury. Where this injury occurs often in high impact sports with an associated sprain, or blow, in swimmers this injury occurs simply from overuse of the joints. Take freestyle for example. At high levels of competition, a swimmer will perform around 12 strokes a length. For each hundred yards, this becomes 48 shoulder rotations. Now this doesn't seem like much but if you multiply this by the number of yards a high caliber swimmer does in a day (15-20k) we get somewhere near ten thousand rotations per day or 3 million rotations per year. This sort of repetition is hard on machines, but swimmers are flesh and blood. Their joints just plain wear out.

In reality, there's no way around it, if you compete as a swimmer and do the training required to reach any level of skill, you will get tendonitis. The only real question is how you're going to respond when you do. The most common joint to get tendonitis as a swimmer is the shoulder, but knee and ankle problems are not unheard of. Within the shoulder, swimmers commonly injure either their bicep tendon or rotator cuff.

How do you know you've got it?

When I first got tendonitis I had no idea what it was. The pain was very like a bee sting. It felt sharp after exercising which transformed into a dull ache. The shoulder felt swollen, less mobile, and weak. Between sets I just started rubbing my shoulder and, I suppose, looking worried. An older swimmer looked to me and said, "First shoulder problem eh? Probably have tendonitis." I looked to the coach who motioned for me to keep swimming and I finished the workout. Afterwards I was initiated into the swimmers injury league, given my bag of ice from the drink machine and told to go take some aspirin. Little did I know it, but I had just entered a fraternity of walking wounded swimmers who would slog to the ice machine after every practice. I had seen these shadowy figures before, exhausted swimmers with strange bulges over their shoulders reading books and chatting while they waited for their medication to kick in. Now I was one of their number and would remain as long as I continued swimming.

What do you do now that you have it?

The most common remedy for shoulder tendonitis is ice and aspirin (or advil, anaprox, or some other nacid) since rest really is not an option for swimmers in training. The ice is supposed to reduce the swelling of the affected tendon while the drug is meant to scour the tendon of any excess scar tissue that might form during recovery (yes it also deadens the pain but that's really just a useful side-effect). You can either massage the tendon with ice for 10 minutes, or so, or put a bag of chipped ice on the area for 20 minutes. Usually this regimen performed after each practice will keep the condition from getting any worse. If not, it's time to go see a doctor and get some physical therapy (PT).

Physical therapists generally have three weapons in their arsenal for attacking a swimmer's tendonitis. The first, and most commonly used is stim. Short for electrical stimulation, the physical therapist puts electrodes on the muscles around the tendon in question and hook them up to a machine. The machine passes a small current of electricity through these electrodes that make your muscles clinch in rhythmic balance, first one side of the tendon will flex, then the other. Usually this goes on for about fifteen minutes then they have you ice and go on your way. It doesn't hurt, and if you can ignore your arm moving of its own accord, pretty restful.

The second method of attacking tendonitis that physical therapists use is ultrasound. The therapist determines the tendon at fault and targets it with a device that looks very similar to the receiver that is put up against an expectant mother's belly when they give her an ultrasound to diagnose any potential issues with her child. Only this ultrasound emitter is a lot more powerful. It's designed to break down the inflammation of the tendon in question with a focused blast of sound waves. Commonly this only really feels warm at the site of the interaction of sound waves and the tissues being treated, but in a very small number of patients, the ultrasonic vibrations can set up a resonance frequency with nearby nerves causing the arm and hand to feel like they're on fire. Boy did I feel lucky.

If stim and ultrasound don't work, the therapist may be asked to manipulate the tendon. When I first heard of this I thought, sure this won't be bad, just move some things around and it'll be over in a snap. My shoulders being so loose as to move about on their own accord already, it didn't seem like a big deal. I was wrong. Manipulation of a tendon refers to the therapist using their hands to forcibly rub the inflammation out of the offending tendon. Typical associated medication with this technique is a rolled up towel to bite down upon since bullets are hard to find in the PT office.

Finally, if stim, ultrasound, and manipulation don't work, the doctor may order a cortisone shot. Cortisone is a steroid used to help tendons and connective tissue repair itself and it can reduce the inflammation of tendonitis drastically. Bring that towel though from the PTs cause this shot isn?t a flu shot. The needle they have to use to get into the joint is about four inches long and feels like liquid fire is being poured into your shoulder. If this doesn't work, there's no remedy other than surgery for repairing your tendons.

How do you make sure you don't get it again?

Given all these "remedies" to shoulder tendonitis, it's no small wonder that swimmers with this problem work like crazy to keep their shoulders fit and able to outlast the punishment of swimming practice. Swimmers' shoulders are commonly very flexible given the demands of their sport. However, that same flexibility leads to shoulder instability and tendon damage. So in order to avoid recurrences of tendonitis, swimmers have developed a regimen of exercises that strengthen the back muscles near the shoulder to help keep it stable during a full stroke rotation. All these exercises are done with small amounts of weight or with surgical tubing to create resistance. They are also done with a high number of repetitions since the idea is to build endurance as well as strength in these muscle groups that are in opposition to those commonly used in swimming.

The first exercise is to lay on your side with one shoulder up. Keep the upper arm at your side and bend your elbow 90 degrees. While holding the weight in your hand, rotate the weight from in front of your belly to over your elbow while keeping that elbow immobilized at your side. After doing about twenty reps, flip over and do the other side. The second exercise is to stand on the floor with your feet shoulder-width apart. Take a small weight in both hands and bend 90 degrees at the waist so that you're facing the floor. Hold the weights straight out toward the floor and while keeping your arms straight and the backs of your hands pointed towards the ceiling, bring those weights to an equal height with your shoulders. Do about twenty reps this way. These and other shoulder exercises will aid in creating a strong foundation for your shoulders so they won't move about as much during your stroke rotation. Less instability in your shoulder socket leads to less likelihood of developing tendonitis.

An ice and aspirin regimen can also be used as a prophylactic measure. Whenever you're done with practice, go get a bag of ice and put it on your shoulder. Take some aspirin. After twenty minutes, take the ice off and stretch out the shoulder lightly. I know this extra 20 minutes out of your day is a burden, especially if you're in school. However, you'll find that it's a worthwhile use of your time considering that the alternative is hours spent in the physical therapist's trying to recover from an injury.

Now, please be advised, I am not a doctor. If anything you're experiencing is worse than what I've described here or if you feel something different, go see a good doctor. Physical therapists also have a wealth of information and exercises that will be tailored to your specific injury so don't be shy in visiting them either. Above all protect your body. It's your only real asset when it comes to this sport.

POOLS

Swimming pools are where all the action happens as a swimmer. You practice there, you compete there, and if you're really serious, you eat, drink, and even sleep there too. A swimming pool is so central to a swimmer's life that many small differences in its design can make a huge difference to how the swimmer needs to approach competition and even practice. In this section I'll discuss every element of the pool's environment and how these elements can affect your performance.

The Competition Pool

POOL CHEMICALS

Since a swimmer spends so much time in the water, the pool chemicals that are used (and often abused) by pool managers as they try to keep the pool water clean from the kids who like to pee in the pool, slowly seep into a swimmer's skin making them have a very distinctive and pervasive odor. Furthermore, these chemicals damage hair and nails, so swimmers who value their appearance tend to have to take extra steps to keep their appearance up to their standards. Swimmers, the masochists that they are, regularly spend up to six hours a day in this caustic environment and would probably do more, if they didn't have to sleep. So how do swimmers put up with it all? Chemical warfare.

If you've ever been underwater at a pool, you know the primary chemical that pools use to keep the water safe from biological contamination; chlorine. If you don't have eye protection, your eyes will start to itch, then burn, and eventually turn so red that Dracula will think you're a long lost relative. Once this happens to you, the thing you must not do is rub your eyes. I know it's like being told not to scratch poison ivy, but rubbing your eyes when they've been exposed to chlorine rubs the chemicals deeper into the tissue around your eyes. You will feel better for a few seconds then they will itch ten times worse. The best thing to do when you feel like your eyes have been exposed to too much chlorine is to run your eyes through water from the tap in the locker room. I know some of you are thinking that's just the hair of the dog that bit you, but the water coming out of the tap in the locker room or from the drinking fountain contains hundredths of the chemical content in the pool water. Once you rinse your eyes out, you'll feel much better and within a few minutes, you'll even look human.

What can you do, though, when the local pool manager has decided to hyper-chlorinate the pool and the air tastes like a chrome tailpipe? Open a door and get some air. Most pools are designed and operated on the behalf of waders. As such, they are frequently treated as toilets by their clientele. Pool managers, who don't get paid if the pool is closed, will put up to 10 times the recommended chlorine into the water in hopes of killing the germs and staying open. Unfortunately, when swimming practice time comes after school, the air has been suffused with a mild mustard gas that burns the lungs of the passer by, and sears the lungs of anyone trying to work out in there. Furthermore, chlorine is heavier than air and as such will tend to gather at the water surface. While the coach (who is frequently the pool manager) is claiming that he can breathe perfectly fine, the swimmer gets to breathe the gas nearest the water as they're swimming along. Once you've been affected by this mustard gas there's really not much you can do besides get clean, fresh air into the pool (and put up with the coughing). The best way to do this is to open all the windows and doors. Even if the air is freezing outside, it's far better to catch cold than ruin your lungs.

Chlorine however is not the only chemical that pool managers use to maintain their pools (and stay on the good side of the health department). Many pools use muriatic and hydrochloric acid in order to keep their pools pristine. These acids work wonders on balancing the water's PH after having to hyper-chlorinate. They are also used to get that stubborn black mildew off of the pool's walls. Unfortunately, they can also damage a swimmers hair, nails and even teeth, if you're not careful. So once a swimmer is done with practice, they'll have to get all those chemicals off their bodies. This is why a swimmer showers.

I know you must be thinking that swimmers spend all their time in the water that's kept clean and fresh for them and then go shower themselves off. They must be the cleanest people in the world, right? Wrong. The chemicals that a swimmer soaks in day after day, leaches calcium from nails, removes oil from hair and skin, breaks down rubber, and destroys lycra and nylon. Swimmers always smell of chlorine, but must shower in order to remove all the acids and chemicals off of their bodies. Now if you care for your hair and nails, you'll have to condition your hair and use vitamin E cream on your nails. Otherwise both become brittle. You may want to drink after swimming because you're thirsty, but that's also a good idea to wash the acids off your teeth so they're not etched by the strong acids in the water.

Another perennial problem that swimmers have is with their skin. Dunking yourself in water repeatedly is a quick way to rob your skin of moisture as the air leaches the moisture away from your body as you dry. The chemical-laden water of swimming pools is even worse. Chlorine strips away a body's natural oil so that when you do get out and dry off, there are fewer oils to keep moisture in your skin. To avoid this, many swimmers use over-the-counter body lotion after drying off to seal in whatever moisture might be left after getting out of the pool and drying off. It's not a perfect solution but it does make you considerably less itchy after practice.

When you spend upwards of six hours in a pool a day, though, there's no way you're going to completely cleanse the chlorine and other chemicals from your body. If you take care of yourself, with conditioner, skin lotion, and showers, you'll avoid most of the most damaging effects of these chemicals.

POOL WALLS

Walls in the real world can make us feel boxed in but walls in a swimming pool can either slow us down or speed us up depending upon how we use them. Depending upon how the wall is made, it will either reflect waves back at a swimmer or swallow them. Swimmers generally prefer walls designed to reduce the waves in a pool, and as such, the best competition pools in the world take this design element into account when they're built. A wave swallowing wall, is either designed to meet the waterline of the pool or have a gutter that meets the waterline so that any waves that are made near the wall, wash into a gutter and do not bounce back to affect the swimmer's performance. Not all walls are designed this way, though so be aware of how the walls interact with waves in the pool as you warm up.

Sooner or later, in everyone's swimming career, you will end up in an outside lane. This lane is so called because it is the outermost lane in the pool. One side of the lane is bounded by a lane-line, the other, by the wall of the pool. These lanes are the least favorite of swimmers because the waves that they create during swimming will bounce off the wall, return, and interfere with their body position. Walls that are designed to swallow waves are more swimmer-friendly, and create less of this problem, but since the swimmer's wake extends below the waterline as well as above it, the wall still creates a problem. Most competitive swimmers in this circumstance will swim on the inside of the lane, the side of the lane where the lane-line is, in order to avoid the interference of their own wake bouncing back off of the wall. This positioning usually solves the majority of the problem. Everyone, however, has to deal with the walls at the ends of the pools. If they don't swallow waves, swimmers have to be extra careful with their wakes.

Pools that do not have wave-swallowing gutters will create a lot of turbulence as swimmers make their turns. A swimmer who does not get to the wall first in one of these pools will have to deal with about two yards of unstable water next to the wall in order to make their turn. The only solution in these pools, is to be first to the wall. If you're first to the wall or within half a bodylength of the lead swimmer, the wake interaction with the wall will not have a chance to churn up the water near the wall before you're off the wall and traveling the other way. If there is a wave swallowing gutter at the wall, though, there won't be anywhere near as much turbulence. Some pools, though don't use gutters to swallow waves on all their walls. They use bulkheads to separate a large pool into smaller competition-length areas.

Most bulkheads used in pools are metal frames with rubberized plastic grating covering their surfaces. As such, they don't just let surface waves through, they let all the waves a swimmer creates through. Unlike the other walls of a pool, there is never any turbulence around these walls and the water around them feels comparatively silky compared to a regular wall. Bulkhead walls will feel sharp on the feet (they may even be a little painful), but with practice they can be used a lot like a trampoline. Bulkheads, by their nature are really only anchored to the sides of the pool, as such, they have a certain amount of give to them, especially in the middle lanes. To get the most benefit out of this springiness, you will want to drive a little closer to the bulkhead wall than you would a normal one. The extra force you get by being an inch or two closer, will make the wall warp and push back with more force, speeding your streamlined turn recovery faster than a solid wall.

Walls are extremely important to all swimmers, but to backstrokers, they are a matter of survival. Since a backstroker cannot see the walls as they approach them, they will need to learn to read the ceiling of every pool they swim in. Luckily, there really are only five or so distinct pool designs out there so once you learn to read these ceilings, you'll have an easier time of knowing where you are in the pool at any given moment. Many of these ceilings have features that, if read correctly, will let the backstroker know when they're close to a wall. My favorite ceilings have always been those made out of corrugated metal. The lines of the metal always match the direction of the pool, so you can easily course correct and keep moving straight without having to look around and through doing so, ruin your body position. Unfortunately one can only learn how to read a pool's ceiling through practice, a relatively painful process since it results in a number of concussions getting it right.

Once as a very young swimmer I undertook a 50 yard backstroke. I was a slower swimmer at the time so I was put in one of the end lanes. I made it to the other end straight and fast, probably faster than I was used to, since I missed my count from the flags and hit my head. Not wanting to disappoint my coach, I made my turn (as only you can when your head is next to the wall and your hand is dangling from your shoulder up over the side of the pool) and started heading back for the last length. I must have been still dazed from the first crack, because on the way back, I hit my head again on the side of the pool. Once the stars stopped spinning, I swerved on to the finish where I promptly forgot again to count my strokes from the flags and hit my head a third time at the end. The official, who did his utmost to do his duty and make sure that I didn't roll over on my front after any of those clunks (it was his job to disqualify me if I did), helped me out of the water and put some ice on my lumps. I'll never forget the look of intense fascination and concern on his face as he hovered right over me during the entire ordeal. I really hope to never see anyone look at me that way again.

It was a matter of survival, then that I learned how to read ceilings as a backstroker and keep my head off the walls. All swimmers, though, can make good use of pool walls to help their performance. Simply avoid the walls when they'll slow you down, and attack them hard when they'll help you. You'll be a better swimmer for it.

WATER DEPTH

Pools come in many shapes and sizes. Their length can vary as well as the water depth. Most competitions happen in either 25 yard pools or 50 meter pools. However, at lower levels of competition many other sizes of pools get used. Pools that are 25 meters long are some of the notable exceptions, but there have even been pools that have been made 100 feet long. Measuring a standard-length competition race can be tricky here since there is frequently not a wall for the swimmers to finish. The one pool I encountered at this length, required us to cross a finish line much like that at a track meet. Though, by far, the hardest job there was done by the timers. They had to stand at the side of the pool all bunched up (three per lane), and guess when a swimmer crossed that imaginary finish line.

A Swimmer's Natural Environment

Considering how many lengths pools come in, it's not much of a surprise then, that pools also come in a variety of depths. Most, being designed for wading and recreation swimming, change depth along their length. These changes of water depth can provide a variety of challenges to competitive swimmers. The best swimming pools in the world for competition swimming are uniformly near nine feet deep. At this depth the wake that a swimmer produces in the act of swimming is weak enough when it reaches the bottom of the pool, that it cannot impact the swimmer, or the water near the swimmer much at all. However, when a pool is shallower, say three or four feet deep, that impact is far greater.

When you watch a swimmer going through the water, you see a wake at the surface of the water, much like that of a boat. Well that wake also continues in three dimensions to the bottom of the pool. Now when you see that swimmer lane one, for instance, his wake bounces off the wall and returns back towards the swimmer. If this swimmer is close to the wall, this wake interferes more with the swimmer than if they are far away. This is why many swimmers who end up in lane one or eight, try to swim on the inside of their lane, to minimize the interference of their own wake. The exact same thing happens under the swimmer as well. In a shallow pool, your wake provides pressure on your body as it bounces back from the bottom of the pool.

When the water is around 5 feet deep, most swimmers may actually feel a benefit from this under-wake. The wake that bounces back from the bottom of the pool hits the swimmer below his waist and he feels like he's swimming downhill. A shallower pool, however will feel very different. The wake from the bottom of the pool hits the swimmer above the waist and makes the swimmer feel like he's swimming uphill.

Many long-course pools (50m pools) have diving wells at one end. When the pool is designed this way, it can start 4 feet deep at one end then progress down to 6 feet near the middle, but soon after that, will drop away to 14 feet or so. The visual cliff a swimmer encounters is not only daunting but can mess with your stroke. As you swim over the edge of this cliff, the wake that you had become used to on the way down the pool, suddenly drops away and your body position completely changes. You'll feel a drop-off in power as you cross this threshold if you don't adjust your body position to the new fluid dynamics.

So how does a swimmer handle these variations in water depth? In shallower pools, make sure that you take off from the walls after a turn, almost completely on your side. This orientation will keep the extra turbulence from your kick from interfering with your progress. You also want to make sure that your body position works with the interference you're getting form your wake bouncing off the bottom of the pool. Generally speaking, the deeper the pool, the higher in the water you'll want to feel in order to get the most benefit.

The diving well cliff though is a real challenge. As you approach the cliff, you will need to adjust your body position drastically because as soon as you cross over the threshold your wake will no longer have any contact with the bottom of the pool. From a normal competition body position, as you cross the threshold, power through the first few strokes over the boundary. Most swimmers will slow down at this point so you'll likely catch them unawares. Once you've done a few power strokes you can go back to what feels like your normal position but you will have made the adjustment.

Very few of us are lucky enough to swim in great swimming pools our entire career. Most of us have to make the cutoff times for the big events in sub-standard pools. The more you plan for the environment that you'll be swimming in, the better you'll do, and the more likely you'll get to swim in the best pools in the world.

WATER TEMPERATURE

All water's the same right? I know there are water bottling companies who have spent a lot of money to tell you that their water is better than any other for drinking, but have you thought about the water you swim in? I didn't think so. Water temperature has a significant effect on a swimmer's performance. If you know how to adapt you will have a leg up on your competition and in the world of swimming where hundredths of a second determine the winner, that could make all the difference.

Most competition swimming pools are kept at 78 degrees Fahrenheit. They're kept cooler than most wading pools which are kept at 82 degrees because the lower temperature keeps the competing swimmers from overheating during their events. Since muscle generated body heat contributes a significant amount to a swimmer's overall fatigue, the cooler the water, the better (to a point). The best competition pools in the world, for instance, are kept at 75 degrees in order to help the swimmers dissipate body heat quicker. I know it sounds strange, but when you're exerting yourself as a swimmer, 78 degrees in the water feels like 75 degrees on land. Every two degree increase in water temperature feels like an increase in five degrees to that swimmer working out. So those pools which are set for waders at 82 degrees, feels like 85, if that water temperature creeps higher to say, 84, it will feel like it's 90 to a working swimmer.

These may seem like small differences, but if you've tried to do a full workout in 85-90 degree weather, you'll know how hard it is to stay on your game. Many pools used by waders predominantly, like YMCAs and the like don't know to change the temperature of their water for a competition, so you will have to take some precautions if the water is this hot. You may not realize it but you will sweat profusely when you swim at a high level. You don't feel it because the water is constantly washing it all away, but in order to stay cool, have some ice water you can sip almost constantly during a meet in a hot pool. Be careful you don't over hydrate though and lose the electrolytes you use to metabolize energy, just drink enough so that you never feel thirsty. Another trick for dealing with hot water, is to find a resting spot between your events either outside or in a cool part of the building. The cooler you can keep your body between events, the less effect the hot water will have on your performance.

Some outdoor pools can get quite cold though and offer a different challenge to a swimmer trying to stay at the top of their game. Water temperatures can be as low as 68 degrees and still be considered viable to be used in a meet. It's not pleasant, but it's not uncommon for this to happen. When this is the case, you will need to keep your body warm and loose in order to perform well. If the pool is this cold, make sure you warm up thoroughly before your event. Once your warm up is done, towel off as fast as you can, get into your sweats and find a warm place to sit, even if it is your car. Have someone come and get you ten minutes before your event so you can get ready. When you do dive into the water for your event, make sure that you stay as loose as possible. I know water this cold feels like hitting a brick wall, but the looser you keep your body as you enter and start your event, the less energy you'll waste on keeping yourself warm and the more energy you can spend on your race.